THE ST ANDREW'S ENCYCLOPEDIA

Other titles available in this series

The Anfield Encyclopedia: an A–Z of Liverpool FC
The Elland Road Encyclopedia: an A–Z of Leeds United FC
The Hawthorns Encyclopedia: an A–Z of West Bromwich Albion FC
The Highbury Encyclopedia: an A–Z of Arsenal FC
The Hillsborough Encyclopedia: an A–Z of Sheffield Wednesday FC
The Maine Road Encyclopedia: an A–Z of Manchester City FC
The Molineux Encyclopedia: an A–Z of Wolverhampton Wanderers
The Old Trafford Encyclopedia: an A–Z of Manchester United FC
The St James's Park Encyclopedia: an A–Z of Newcastle United FC
The Stamford Bridge Encyclopedia: an A–Z of Chelsea FC
The Villa Park Encyclopedia: an A–Z of Aston Villa FC
The White Hart Lane Encyclopedia: an A–Z of Tottenham Hotspur FC

THE ST ANDREW'S ENCYCLOPEDIA

An A-Z of Birmingham City

Dean Hayes

MAINSTREAM
PUBLISHING

EDINBURGH AND LONDON

To all St Andrew's fans everywhere!

Copyright © Dean Hayes, 1999
All rights reserved
The moral right of the author has been asserted

First published in Great Britain in 1999 by
MAINSTREAM PUBLISHING COMPANY (EDINBURGH) LTD
7 Albany Street
Edinburgh EH1 3UG

ISBN 1 84018 141 9

No part of this book may be reproduced or transmitted in any form or by any means without written permission from the publisher, except by a reviewer who wishes to quote brief passages in connection with a review written for insertion in a magazine, newspaper or broadcast

The photographs in this book have been kindly supplied by the *Lancashire Evening Post*, the *Stockport Express Advertiser* and the *Birmingham Post* and *Mail*.

A catalogue record for this book is available from the British Library

Typeset in Janson Text
Printed and bound in Great Britain by The Cromwell Press

A

ABANDONED MATCHES Generally speaking, far fewer matches are abandoned than previously because if there is some doubt about the ability to play the full game, the match is likely to be postponed. In 1882 the Blues were leading Darlaston All Saints 16–0. They had scored eight of the goals in the first quarter of an hour of the second half when, with a little under 30 minutes still left to play, the referee called the game off!

ABBOTT, WALTER Walter Abbott made a goalscoring début for the Blues against Manchester City at Muntz Street in a Test match in April 1896, just days after joining the Heathens from Rosewood Victoria. After scoring four goals in 12 games in 1896–97, he topped the Blues' scoring charts for the next two seasons with a club record of 42 goals in just 40 league and cup games in 1898–99. That season he scored five goals in the 8–0 defeat of Darwen and hat-tricks against Loughborough Town (Home 6–0), Woolwich Arsenal (Home 4–1) and Gainsborough Trinity (Home 6–1). At the end of that season he was allowed to join Everton where he was switched from inside-forward to left-half and went on to play in 291 league and cup games, scoring 37 goals for the Merseyside club. Surprisingly, Abbott's only England cap saw him play at centre-half in a goalless draw against Wales at Wrexham in 1902. He played in Everton's two FA Cup final appearances of 1906 and 1907, picking up a winners' medal in the first of those finals as the Goodison club beat Newcastle United 1–0. He left Everton in the close season of 1908 and joined Burnley before returning to play for Small Heath. Sadly, after scoring 66 goals in 85 games, he was forced to retire with a knee injury.

ABLETT, GARY The Liverpool-born defender joined his home-town club, but made his Football League début at Bournemouth whilst on loan for Derby County in January 1985. He also had further league experience with Hull City before returning to Anfield and playing his first game for the Reds in December 1986. It was midway through the following season that he established himself in the Liverpool first team and in 1989 he won an FA Cup winners' medal as Everton were beaten 3–2. He also won two League Championship medals with the club in 1987–88 and 1989–90 but, after playing in 147 first-team games, he was allowed to join Merseyside rivals, Everton, for £750,000. He soon settled down at Goodison Park, playing at both left-back and in the centre of defence but, with increased competition, he lost his place halfway through the 1995–96 season and went on loan to Sheffield United. Though the Blades tried to sign him on a permanent basis, it was Birmingham City who secured his services for £400,000 in June 1996 after he had appeared in 156 games for Everton. He made his City début in a 1–0 home win over Crystal Palace on the opening day of the 1996–97 season and went on to appear in 42 league games which won him the Blues' Clubman of the Year award, decided by manager Trevor Francis. He continues to play to a high standard for the St Andrew's club and has now appeared in well over 100 games for the club.

ADEBOLA, DELE The Nigerian-born striker began his Football League career with Crewe Alexandra where, despite having two spells out through injury, he was the club's leading scorer in 1996–97 with 18 goals to his credit as the Gresty Road club moved into the First Division for the first time in its history. He had scored 46 goals in 152 games for the Railwaymen when the Blues paid £1 million to take him to St Andrew's. Deceptively fast for a big man, he made his City début as a substitute in a 1–1 home draw against Middlesbrough on 7 February 1998. The following week he returned to Gresty Road and scored Birmingham's first goal in a 2–0 win. He scored five goals in seven starts and his partnership with Peter Ndlovu steered the Blues towards the play-offs where they lost out on goal difference to Sheffield United. In 1998–99, Adebola was in great form and was instrumental in the club lying in a play-off place at the time of writing.

Alan Ainscow

AGGREGATE SCORES Birmingham City's highest aggregate score in any competition came in the Inter Cities Fairs Cup competition of 1960–61. Playing Boldklub Copenhagen of Denmark, the Blues notched up nine goals over the two legs. After a 4–4 draw in Denmark in which Johnny Gordon and James

Singer scored two goals apiece, the St Andrew's side then won 5–0 at home with Robin Stubbs grabbing two of the goals. In the Football League Cup of 1983–84, the Blues beat Derby County 7–0 on aggregate with Mick Harford grabbing a second-leg hat-trick in a 4–0 win at St Andrew's.

AINSCOW, ALAN Bolton-born midfielder Alan Ainscow joined Blackpool as an apprentice in the summer of 1971. In the Anglo–Italian final against Bologna in 1971, still without a league appearance, he played the game of his life for the Seasiders before being substituted at the end of normal time due to exhaustion. He scored on his league début for the Bloomfield Road club in a 4–1 home win over Swindon Town on the opening day of the 1971–72 season. After Tommy Hutchison had left the club, Ainscow became a virtual ever-present and, over the next seven seasons, scored 28 goals in 209 first-team appearances before being transferred to Birmingham City in July 1978. He made his début for the Blues in a 1–0 defeat against Manchester United at Old Trafford on the opening day of the 1978–79 season, going on to appear in 31 games during that relegation campaign. The following season the club returned to the top flight at the first attempt with Ainscow scoring six goals in 37 games. In fact, whenever he scored, the Blues won! He missed just two games in 1980–81, as the club finished thirteenth in the First Division, before leaving to play for Everton. Ainscow later had short spells with Barnsley (on loan), Wolves and Blackburn Rovers as well as playing in Hong Kong.

ANGLO–ITALIAN CUP When Swindon Town won the Football League Cup in 1969 they were ineligible for the Fairs Cup because they were not a First Division side. Consequently they organised a match against the Italian League Cup winners, AS Roma, and played for the Anglo–Italian League Cup. The following year the Anglo–Italian Cup was introduced for club sides from the two countries who had no involvement in Europe. The Blues first entered at the end of the 1971–72 season. Their results were:

Lanerossi Vicenza	Home 5–3	Away 0–0
Sampdoria	Home 2–0	Away 1–2

They finished fourth in the English group and failed to qualify for the final. The Blues next entered the much maligned competition in 1992–93 when, after beating Sunderland (Away 1–0) and drawing with Cambridge United (Home 3–3), they qualified for the international stage of the competition. Their results were as follows:

AS Bari	Home 1–0	AC Cesena	Away 2–1
Lucchese	Away 0–3	Ascoli Calcio	Home 1–1

In 1993–94, the Blues lost 2–0 at Stoke City and drew 2–2 at home to Wolverhampton Wanderers, when substitute Adam Wratten scored both goals, but failed to qualify for the international stage. The club did not enter the competition in 1994–95 but returned the following season with the competition reduced to eight invited clubs from each country. City's results were as follows:

Genoa	Home 2–3	Perugia	Away 1–0
Ancona	Away 2–1	Cesena	Home 3–1

In the domestic semi–final, the Blues were held to a 2–2 draw at St Andrew's by West Bromwich Albion before losing 4–1 on penalties.

ANGLO–SCOTTISH CUP The qualifying stages of this competition took place during the pre-season on a league basis with the qualifying clubs going through to face Scottish opposition on a two-legged basis. Sadly, the Blues never reached that stage, for in 1977–78 their results were: Plymouth Argyle (Away 1–1), Bristol Rovers (Away 1–1) and Bristol City (Home 1–0) and in 1979–80, Bristol City (Home 0–4), Plymouth Argyle (Away 1–1) and Fulham (Away 5–0).

APPEARANCES Gil Merrick holds the record for the number of first team appearances in a Birmingham City shirt, with a total of 541 games to his credit between 1946 and 1959. The players with the highest number of appearances are as follows:

	League	FA Cup	FLg Cup	Others	Total
1. Gil Merrick	485	56	0	0	541
2. Frank Womack	491	24	0	0	515
3. Joe Bradford	414	31	0	0	445
4. Ken Green	401	35	0	6	442
5. Johnny Crosbie	409	23	0	0	432
6. Trevor Smith	365	35	12	18	430
7. Malcolm Beard	350(1)	24(1)	25	4	403(2)
8. Dan Tremelling	382	13	0	0	395
9. Harry Hibbs	358	30	0	0	388
10. Malcolm Page	328(11)	29	14	12	383(11)

ARCHER, ARTHUR Derby-born full-back Arthur Archer played his early football with Burton St Edmunds, Tutbury Hampton and Burton Wanderers before joining the Blues in the summer of 1897. His first game for the club was in the opening match of the 1897–98 season as the Blues won 3–1 at Burton Swifts. Forming a good full–back partnership with William Pratt, Archer missed just one game that campaign and, in five seasons with the club, he was ever-present in 1899–1900 and 1900–01 when he appeared in 96 consecutive league games. In 1900–01 the club won promotion to the First Division with Archer scoring two goals – the winner at Middlesbrough and the opening goal in the 10–1 rout of Blackpool. He went on to score four goals in 170 games before joining New Brompton in 1902. At the end of the following season he was transferred to Queen's Park Rangers before moving to Norwich City in August 1905. He later played for Brighton before ending his career with Millwall.

ASTALL, GORDON Born at Horwich near Bolton, winger Gordon Astall began his career as an amateur with Southampton before joining Plymouth Argyle while serving with the Royal Marines. In six seasons at Home Park, Astall scored 42 goals in 188 league games before being transferred to Birmingham City in October 1953. His first game for the Blues was in a 1–1 draw at Bristol Rovers, after which he soon settled into the St Andrew's side, teaming up with Noel Kinsey in the Birmingham attack. He was an important member of the Blues' Second Division Championship-winning side of 1954–55, scoring 11 goals in 33 games. In 1955–56 he had his best goal-scoring season when he netted 12 league goals and another 3 in the club's run to the FA Cup final, including one in the semi-final victory over Sunderland. His form that season earned him international recognition when he won two full caps for England against Finland and West Germany. A member of the City side that lost to Barcelona in the final of the Inter Cities Fairs Cup, he went on to score 67 goals in 271 league and cup games before leaving St Andrew's to join Torquay United, where he took his tally of league goals to 112, a good return for a winger.

ATHERSMITH, CHARLIE One of the game's fastest wingers, Charlie Athersmith spent the 1890s with Aston Villa, scoring 85 goals in 308 league and cup matches. He joined Villa from Unity Gas Depot FC, making his league début at home to Preston North End in May 1891, a month before John Devey was signed. Devey and Athersmith formed an outstanding right-wing partnership, one which helped to make Athersmith a supreme footballer. Athersmith was rewarded with two FA Cup winners' medals, five League Championship winners' medals and 12 England caps, as well as nine appearances for the Football League. In Villa's double season of 1896–97, he won every honour available, adding England caps against Scotland, Wales and Ireland to his double medals. After leaving Villa Park in the summer of 1901, he joined the Blues. His first game for the club was in a 4–1 win at Manchester City on 14 September 1901 when he helped to create all of the club's goals. Though the Blues were relegated at the end of his first season with the club, they returned to the top flight in 1902–03 as runners-up to Manchester City in a closely fought Second Division promotion race. He had scored 13 goals in 106 games when he left the game in the summer of 1905, returning two years later as Grimsby Town's trainer.

ATKINS, ARTHUR Though he was born in Tokyo where his parents were in business, centre-half Arthur Atkins was brought up in Erdington and discovered by the St Andrew's club whilst playing for Paget Rangers. He made his début for the Blues at home to Burnley in September 1949 and he went on to make 20 appearances in that campaign. In 1950–51 he was one of three ever-presents in a Birmingham side that finished fourth in Division Two. In addition, he was outstanding that season in the club's run to the semi-finals of the FA Cup where they lost to Blackpool after a replay. He went on to appear in 105 games for the Blues but, after losing his place to Trevor Smith, he left St Andrew's and joined Shrewsbury Town. After just one season at Gay Meadow he left to play non-league football.

ATTENDANCE – AVERAGE The average home-league attendances of Birmingham City over the last ten seasons have been as follows:

1988–89	6,265	1993–94	14,506
1989–90	8,558	1994–95	16,983
1990–91	7,030	1995–96	18,090
1991–92	12,400	1996–97	17,751
1992–93	12,328	1997–98	18,708

ATTENDANCE – HIGHEST The record attendance at St Andrew's is 66,844 for the fifth-round FA Cup game with Everton on 11 February 1939. The match ended in a 2–2 draw but City lost the replay at Goodison Park four days later 2–1.

ATTENDANCE – LOWEST The lowest attendance at St Andrew's is 1,500 for Chesterfield's visit on 17 April 1909. The Blues won 3–0 with Arthur Mounteney scoring a hat-trick.

AULD, BERTIE Glasgow-born Bertie Auld signed professional forms for Celtic in March 1955 and, after spending much of the 1956–57 season on loan at Dumbarton, settled into the Parkhead club's side. With Celtic he won three Scottish caps, the first against Hungary in 1959. In April 1961 he left the Scottish giants to sign for Birmingham City for a fee of £15,000 and made his début in the Inter Cities Fairs Cup semi-final second leg when the Blues beat Internazionale at St Andrew's 2–1. He made his league début in a 2–1 home win over Fulham on the opening day of the 1961–62 campaign and over the next three and a half seasons was a regular member of the Birmingham side. In 1962–63 he scored some vital goals in the club's run to the League Cup final where they beat Aston Villa over two legs. The following season he was the club's top scorer with 10 league goals – but early in 1965, after netting 31 goals in 145 games, he returned to Celtic for £12,000.

Jock Stein converted him from a winger to a thoughtful, intelligent midfielder – the transformation was quite staggering and saw him become part of the great Celtic side that won the European Cup in 1967. He left Parkhead in 1971 to play briefly for Hibernian before becoming coach at Easter Road. He later managed Partick Thistle (twice), Hibs, Hamilton Academical and Dumbarton.

AUTOGLASS TROPHY The Autoglass Trophy replaced the Leyland Daf Cup for the 1991–92 season. Birmingham failed to qualify for the knockout stages after losing both of the preliminary round matches, 3–1 at Stoke City and 1–0 at home to Walsall.

AUTO WINDSCREEN SHIELD The Auto Windscreen Shield replaced the Autoglass Trophy for the 1994–95 season. City's first match saw them beat Peterborough United 5–3 at London Road with Jonathan Hunt grabbing a hat-trick. There then followed victories over Walsall (Home 3–0), Gillingham (Home 3–0) and Hereford United (Home 3–1) before the Blues met Swansea City in the Southern Area semi-final. With the scores level at 2–2 after extra-time, substitute Tait scored the 'sudden death' winner that took the St Andrew's club into the Southern Area final against Leyton Orient. A Peter Shearer goal gave Birmingham a 1–0 win at St Andrew's, whilst in the second leg, at Brisbane Road, two goals from Steve Claridge gave City a 3–2 win on the night, 4–2 on aggregate. In the final, the Blues met Carlisle United at Wembley. A crowd of 76,663 witnessed a poor match which was goalless after extra-time. The 'sudden death' rule came into play and from Ricky Otto's chipped pass, Paul Tait scored the all-important goal for the Blues.

AWAY MATCHES Birmingham City's best away win is 7–0, a scoreline achieved in two league games, against Northwich Victoria in 1893–94 and Stoke City in 1997–98. The club have also scored seven goals away from home on three other occasions, beating Leicester City 7–3 in 1933–34, Torquay United 7–1 in their run to the FA Cup final in 1955–56, and Nottingham Forest 7–1 in 1958–59. The Blues' worst defeat away from home is 9–1, a scoreline by which the club have been beaten on two occasions in the Football League – Blackburn Rovers in 1894–95 and Sheffield Wednesday in 1930–31. The highest-scoring away match that the Blues have been involved in was in 1929–30 when they lost 7–5 to Blackburn Rovers at Ewood Park.

AWAY SEASONS The club's highest number of away wins came in 1984–85 when they won 13 of their 21 matches when winning promotion to the First Division. The Blues' fewest away wins (one) occurred in seasons 1909–10, 1949–50 and 1978–79. In this latter season the club's only success came in the final game of the campaign when they won 3–1 at Queen's Park Rangers.

B

BADHAM, JACK One of the club's greatest utility players, Jack Badham played in eight different positions for the Blues in his 10 seasons at St Andrew's. He joined the club from Muntz Street Youth Club and joined the professional ranks in the summer of 1946 after serving in the armed forces. He made his début in a 3–0 win at Chesterfield in February 1948 but played in just one more match that season as the Blues won the Second Division Championship. He established himself as a first-team regular midway through the 1948–49 season and went on to appear in two FA Cup semi–finals with the Blues in 1951 and 1956 and help the club win promotion to the First Division again in 1954–55. A loyal one-club man, Badham never complained when he was omitted from the Blues' line-up for the 1956 FA Cup final against Manchester City. A great crowd favourite, he had appeared in 190 first-team games when he hung up his boots in 1959 to become manager of Birmingham League club, Moor Green.

BALL, BILLY Full-back Billy Ball had played his early football with Stourbridge and Leamington but was with Wellington Town when the Blues persuaded him to join them in the summer of 1911. He made his league début in a 3–2 home defeat by Bradford on the opening day of the 1911–12 season, and by the outbreak of the First World War he had appeared in 138 games for the club. In 1919–20 he played for England against Wales in a Victory International and, the following season, his last with the club when he took his total appearances to 165, he helped the Blues win the Second Division Championship. One of the few players to have represented the club on either side of the First World War, he left St Andrew's in 1921 to end his career with one of his former clubs, Wellington Town.

BARKAS, NED Born at Wardley, Northumberland, full-back Ned Barkas worked as a collier and played non-league football for a number of local sides before joining Huddersfield Town in 1921. During his time with the Terriers, Barkas won two League Championship medals in 1924 and 1926 and was captain of the Yorkshire club which lost 3–1 to Blackburn Rovers in the FA Cup final of 1928. Barkas left Leeds Road to join Birmingham in 1928. His first game for the Blues was in a 3–2 win at Manchester City whilst his first goal for the club came from the penalty-spot in his next match at St Andrew's in which his former club Huddersfield Town won 2–1. Barkas was also captain of the Blues when they lost 2–1 to West Bromwich Albion in the FA Cup final of 1931. He had appeared in 288 first-team games for Birmingham when in May 1937 he signed for Chelsea. His manager at Stamford Bridge was Leslie Knighton who had also been Birmingham's boss when Barkas joined the Blues. He made just 28 league appearances for Chelsea before entering non-league football as player–manager of Solihull Town.

BARTON, PERCY Percy Barton joined Birmingham in the summer of 1913 but had to wait until January 1914 before making his first-team début in a 2–1 home win over Notts County. In 1914–15 he missed just one game, showing his versatility towards the end of that campaign when he played at left-back, centre-half, left-half and centre-forward. Though the First World War interrupted his career, he was to be a regular member of the Birmingham side for a further nine seasons after the hostilities had ended. Now playing the majority of his games at left-half, Barton helped the Blues win the Second Division Championship in 1920–21, his performances earning him the first of seven full caps for England when he played against Belgium in May 1921. Though he didn't score too many goals for the Blues, one during that Championship-winning season was a headed goal from fully 30 yards in the 4–1 home win over Wolverhampton Wanderers. A keen, competitive player, Barton was sent off three times in a Birmingham career which saw him score 14 goals in 349 league and cup games.

BEARD, MALCOLM An England Youth international trialist, Beard made his début for the Blues in a 2–1 defeat at Burnley in

September 1960 and, though he only appeared in three games that season, he was ever present in 1961–62 as the club finished seventeenth in the First Division. That season also saw him score his first goal for the club, which in the final game of the campaign City lost 3–2 at home to Spurs. In 1962–63 he helped the Blues win the League Cup, beating Aston Villa in the final. He also appeared in two semi-finals for the club – against Queen's Park Rangers in the League Cup of 1966–67 and against West Bromwich Albion in the FA Cup of 1967–68. He went on to score 32 goals in 405 league and cup games for Birmingham, being sent off in his last game for the club on 5 December 1970 in a 2–1 defeat at Millwall. After leaving St Andrew's, he had a short spell with Aston Villa but spent most of his time in the club's reserve side before playing non-league football for Atherstone. A year later he had become coach to the World Sporting Academy in Saudi Arabia. In 1974 he returned to St Andrew's as scout, a position he later held at Villa Park before becoming coach at Middlesbrough.

BEASLEY, PAT Pat Beasley joined his home-town club Stourbridge before being transferred to Arsenal as a 17 year old in the summer of 1931. Playing primarily as a winger, he was restricted to reserve-team football due to the consistency of Hulme and Bastin, but in 1933–34 he won a regular place and helped the club win the League Championship. He went on to score 24 goals in 89 league and cup games before joining Huddersfield Town for £750 in October 1936. In the three seasons leading up to the Second World War, he appeared in over 100 league games for the Terriers, was a member of their 1937–38 FA Cup final team and won an England cap, scoring the winning goal against Scotland. During the hostilities he 'guested' for Arsenal and won two wartime caps but in December 1945 he left Huddersfield to join Fulham. In his four seasons at Craven Cottage he made over 150 league appearances and helped the Cottagers to the Second Division Championship in 1948–49. He became player–manager of Bristol City in 1950, spending two seasons at Ashton Gate before finishing his playing career to concentrate on management. In January 1958 he joined Birmingham City, initially as joint-manager with Arthur Turner. In September 1958 he became acting manager and then team manager four months later. He left St Andrew's in May 1960 and after a spell as Fulham's scout, managed non-league Dover for four years.

BEER, BILLY Wing-half Billy Beer joined the Blues from Sheffield United in February 1902 after having played in over 100 games for the Blades. He also won an FA Cup winners' medal in 1899 when the Yorkshire side beat Derby County 4–1. Only allowed to leave Bramall Lane because the United board thought he was over the hill, Beer went on to score 35 goals in 250 games for the Blues! The first of these games was against his former club at Bramall Lane, a match the Blues won 4–1. Beer, who was the club's regular penalty-taker and never missed from the spot, retired in 1910 and emigrated to Australia where he spent ten years sheep farming. After returning to the Midlands he became licensee of the Lower Grounds public house, only a stone's throw from Villa Park, and in 1923 was approached by Frank Richards to become manager at St Andrew's. Beer accepted and managed team affairs whilst Richards carried out secretarial duties. Famous for his rigorous training routines, Beer signed a number of new players but the best position the club achieved in his time in charge was eighth in Division One in 1924–25. Beer resigned his post in March 1927 despite a vote of confidence from the Birmingham directors.

BELL, WILLIE Willie Bell joined Queen's Park from Neilston Juniors in 1957 after rejecting an offer from Stoke City. He completed an engineering apprenticeship and won two Scottish Amateur caps before leaving to join Leeds United in the summer of 1960. At Elland Road he was successfully converted into one of the best full-backs the Yorkshire club ever had. He won a Second Division Championship medal in 1963–64 and appeared in the 1965 FA Cup final. He was capped twice by Scotland against Brazil and Portugal in 1966 and, in September 1967, after appearing in 260 league and cup games, he joined Leicester City for £45,000. Two years later he signed for Brighton before retiring to take up coaching. He coached at St Andrew's under his former Leeds United colleague Freddie Goodwin but when Goodwin left the club, he was put in charge of team affairs. He was appointed manager in September 1975 after the Blues had beaten Newcastle United 3–2. At the end of his first season in charge, the club only just avoided the drop, finishing one place above the relegation zone. There was an improvement the following season as the club finished at mid-table but, after they had lost their first five games of the 1977–78 campaign, he lost his job. He took over as manager of Lincoln City but in October 1978 he left to join a religious sect in the USA called the Campus Crusade for Christ. He later coached at Liberty Baptist College in Virginia.

BENNETT, IAN Goalkeeper Ian Bennett joined Newcastle United from Queen's Park Rangers juniors in March 1989 but after being unable to break into the Magpies' first team, he was allowed to join Peterborough United on a free transfer. He had made 89 first-team appearances for 'The Posh' when the Blues paid £325,000 for his services in December 1993. He made his début in a 2–0 home win over West Bromwich Albion and played in 22 games until the end of the season when the club were relegated to the Second Division. In 1994–95, Bennett was ever present, keeping 19 clean sheets, seven in succession (nine including cup games), as the Blues won the Second Division Championship. He also helped the club win the Autowindscreen Shield at Wembley when they beat Carlisle United 1–0 in the final. He started the 1995–96 season where he'd left off, his superb reflexes and agility bringing the Premier League scouts to St Andrew's. Without doubt one of the best shot-stoppers outside the top flight, he has, at the time of writing, appeared in 222 first-team games for the Blues.

BERRY, JOHNNY Johnny Berry was a brilliant winger who was discovered by former Blues' half-back Fred Harris when they played together in the army. Though he signed professional forms for the St Andrew's club in December 1944 he did not get a chance to play in the club's league side until September 1947 when he played in a 1–0 defeat at Newcastle United. He established himself in the Birmingham side midway through the following campaign and in the club's relegation season of 1949–50 missed just three games. He was ever present in 1950–51 as the Blues finished fourth in Division Two but in September 1951, Matt Busby signed him for Manchester United for £25,000 as a replacement for Irish international Jimmy Delaney. At the end of his first season at Old Trafford, the Aldershot-born winger won a League Championship medal. When United next won the title in 1955–56, Berry and Roger Byrne were the only survivors from the previous Championship success. Berry won four full international caps for England before the Munich air disaster ended his career. The injuries he received in the crash meant that he never played again.

BERTSCHIN, KEITH A member of Ipswich Town's FA Youth Cup-winning side of 1975, he scored with his first kick in league football when he made his début for the Portman Road club against Arsenal at Highbury in April 1976. He joined Birmingham City for a fee of £100,000 in the summer of 1977 and made his début in the opening match of the 1977–78 season in a game City lost 4–1 at home to Manchester United. Forming a prolific goalscoring partnership with Trevor Francis, Bertschin was ever present in that campaign, scoring 11 goals and making many more for the Blues' current manager. He broke the same leg twice whilst at St Andrew's, but bounced back each time and in 1979–80 he helped the club win promotion to the First Division. He was the club's leading scorer with 12 goals, a total which included hat-tricks against Luton Town (Away 3–2) and Orient (Home 3–1). He had scored 41 goals in 141 games before signing for Norwich City in August 1981 for £200,000. He helped the Canaries win promotion in his first season at Carrow Road. He went on to score 38 goals in 138 league and cup games before joining Stoke City. He later played for Sunderland, Walsall, Chester City and Aldershot where a foot injury ended his league career.

BEST STARTS The Blues were unbeaten for the first 15 games of the 1900–01 Second Division promotion-winning season when they won eight and drew seven of their matches. Their first defeat came at home to Burnley on 22 December 1900 when they went down 1–0.

BLOOMFIELD, JIMMY Jimmy Bloomfield started his career with Hayes before signing for Brentford in October 1952. After he had completed his National Service, Arsenal paid Brentford £8,000 for his services in July 1954. He became a regular in the Gunners' first team in 1955–56 and was ever present in the side during

Keith Bertschin

1956–57. Around this time he represented the England Under-23 side, won Football League honours and played for London against Barcelona in the 1958 Fairs Cup final. He had scored 56 goals in 227 league and cup games when he was transferred to Birmingham City for £15,000 in November 1960. He made his début for the Blues in a 6–0 defeat at Tottenham Hotspur but held his place for the remaining 25 games of the season. In 1961–62 he had his best season for the club in terms of goals scored, netting

11 times in 35 league games. He won a League Cup winners' medal in 1963 but in the summer of 1964 he returned to Brentford after scoring 32 goals in 148 games. He spent a short time at West Ham United and Plymouth Argyle before finishing his league career at Leyton Orient. He managed Orient from 1967 to 1971 before taking over at Leicester City, whom he managed from 1971 to 1977. He produced entertaining sides at Filbert Street but never gained success. He returned to Orient for a second spell as manager and in 1978 took the club into their first-ever FA Cup semi-final. On leaving Brisbane Road he became a scout for Luton Town but died suddenly at the age of 49 from a heart condition.

BODLE, HAROLD Doncaster-born inside-forward Harold Bodle played his early football for Ridgehill Athletic before signing for Rotherham United. After two seasons at Millmoor in which he failed to establish himself as a first-team regular, he joined Birmingham. He made his début for the Blues in a 1–1 home draw against Grimsby Town which was his only game in the last peacetime season before the Second World War. During the hostilities, Bodle 'guested' for both Doncaster Rovers and Rotherham United and made 83 appearances for the Blues, scoring 34 goals. In 1946–47, Bodle scored 15 goals in 36 league games including a hat-trick in a 6–1 home win over Plymouth Argyle. The following season he was the club's top scorer with 14 league goals as they won the Second Division Championship. He had scored 36 goals in 110 league and cup games when he left St Andrew's to play for Bury. He netted 40 goals in 119 league games for the Shakers before joining Stockport County in October 1952. After just one season at Edgeley Park he signed for Accrington Stanley, ending his league career with the Peel Park club which left the Football League in 1962. He later became manager of non-league Burton Albion.

BOND, JOHN John Bond made his name as an outspoken manager after a career as a full-back for West Ham United and Torquay United. At Upton Park he developed into a steady, skilful defender who could read the game well and was a dead-ball expert. He scored eight goals in the Hammers' Second Division championship side of 1958–59 and played in the club's 1964 FA

John Bond

Cup final victory over Preston North End. At Torquay he helped them to promotion to Division Three before his retirement in 1969. He went into management, first with Bournemouth and then Norwich City, winning success for both clubs. In October 1980 he accepted an offer to join Manchester City. When he arrived at Maine Road, the club were bottom of the First Division without a win. They then won 10 of their next 15 games, ended the season in mid-table and reached the FA Cup final against Spurs and the League Cup semi-final against Liverpool. However, in February 1983 and with Second Division football looming, Bond resigned. After that, he managed Burnley and Swansea before taking charge at Birmingham City in January 1986. When he arrived at St Andrew's, the Blues were in dire straits: they had played 18 games without a win and lost in the FA Cup to non-league Altrincham. He was unable to halt the club's relegation to the Second Division and after another season of struggle, he was sacked in May 1987. He returned to the game two years later as assistant manager at Shrewsbury, succeeding Asa Hartford early in 1990. After the Gay Meadow club failed to make the Third Division play-offs in 1993, he resigned.

BOYD, LEN Len Boyd began his Football League career with Plymouth Argyle, whom he joined following the recommendation of a supporter who saw him playing soccer for the Royal Navy in Malta. Able to play in either of the wing-half positions, he had scored five goals in 78 league games when Birmingham paid £17,000 to bring him to St Andrew's in January 1949. Signed as a replacement for Frank Mitchell who had joined Chelsea, Boyd made his début in a goalless draw at Preston North End. It was midway through the 1949–50 season before he won a regular place in the Blues' side but, following that, he missed very few games over the next seven seasons. His performances led to him winning international recognition when he played for England at 'B' level. Boyd captained the Blues to the Second Division Championship in 1954–55 and at Wembley in the 1956 FA Cup final, going on to score 15 goals in 281 league and cup games before hanging up his boots.

BRADFORD, JOE Born at Peggs Green, Leicester, he once scored 14 goals in a match for his village team against Birstall Rovers, his goalscoring instincts leading to trials for both Aston Villa and Derby County. However, it was Birmingham who signed him, paying Peggs Green £100 for his services and a further £25 when he made his début. He played his first game for the Blues on Christmas Day 1920, scoring Birmingham's goal in a 1–1 draw at West Ham United. Able to play at either centre or inside-forward, he possessed remarkable shooting powers. Though he only played in 17 league games in 1921–22, he was the club's joint-top scorer with 10 goals. The following season he topped the Blues' scoring charts with 18 league goals, a feat he was to achieve on nine occasions. His form led to him winning full international honours for England and in October 1923 he made the first of 12 appearances for his country against Ireland. He scored the first of 12 hat-tricks in November 1924 as the Blues beat Liverpool 5–2 at St Andrew's. In 1925–26 his total of 26 goals in 32 league games included hat-tricks against Spurs (Home 3–1) and Blackburn Rovers (Away 4–4). His best season for the Blues in terms of goals scored was 1927–28 when he netted 32 goals in 40 games including all four in another 4–4 draw at Blackburn Rovers and a hat-trick in a 4–0 home win over Burnley. Two more hat-tricks followed in 1928–29 in wins over Sunderland (Away 4–3) and Leeds United (Home 5–1). In September 1929, Bradford scored 11 goals in the space of eight days – three for Birmingham in a 5–1 home win over Newcastle United, five for the Football League against the Irish League and three for the Blues in a remarkable 7–5 defeat at Blackburn! That season also saw him score further hat-tricks against West Ham United (Home 4–2) and Leicester City (Home 3–0). There is no doubt that he enjoyed playing against Blackburn Rovers and, in 1930–31, he netted another four goals against the Lancashire club in a 4–1 home win. He also scored in that season's FA Cup final, but the Blues lost 2–1 to West Bromwich Albion. The greatest goalscorer in the club's history, he had netted 267 goals in 445 games, including 249 in the Football League when he left St Andrew's to play for Bristol City. After just one season at Ashton Gate he retired to become a café owner and later owned a sports shop with Villa's Eric Houghton. In 1946–47 he scouted for Arsenal and in the late 1960s worked in Birmingham's pools office.

BREMNER, DES Beginning his professional career at Easter Road, midfielder Des Bremner played in 255 first-team games for Hibernian before joining Aston Villa for £250,000 in September 1979, with Joe Ward going in the opposite direction. Whilst with Hibernian, Bremner represented the Scottish League; he won nine Under-23 caps and in 1976 won his only Scottish cap, coming on as a substitute for Kenny Dalglish in the match against

Des Bremner

Switzerland. He also gained runners–up medals in the Scottish League Cup final of 1975 and the Scottish Cup final of 1979. After making his Villa début in a goalless draw against Arsenal, he went on to appear in 107 consecutive league games before he was injured in a 3–1 win over Wolves in March 1982. During that run Villa won the League Championship – and with Bremner's tireless play a great feature of their game, they went on to win the European Cup and European Super Cup. In October 1984 after appearing in 226 first-team games, he moved to Birmingham City for £25,000. He made his début in a 1–0 home win over Huddersfield Town and went on to appear in 30 league games as the Blues won promottion to the First Division as runners-up to champions Oxford United. Over the next five seasons, Bremner was a first-team regular at St Andrew's, playing in 195 games for the club. He later played for Fulham and Walsall before ending his career with Stafford Rangers.

BRENNAN, BOBBY Belfast-born inside-forward Bobby Brennan began his footballing career with Distillery where he won an Irish Cup runners-up medal and represented the Irish League. In October 1947 he joined Luton Town for £3,000 and had scored 22 goals in 67 league appearances when he left Kenilworth Road to sign for Birmingham City for £20,000 in the summer of 1949. He made his City début in a 3–0 home defeat by Chelsea on the opening day of the 1949–50 season and went on to appear in 39 games, scoring seven goals. Sadly, the Blues were relegated after finishing bottom of the First Division and Brennan left to join Fulham for £19,500. Having added three more Northern Ireland caps to his tally whilst at St Andrew's, he spent three years at Craven Cottage before signing for Norwich City in the summer of 1953. He scored the only goal of the game on his début for the Canaries in a 1–0 win over Southend United and after ending the season as the club's joint-top scorer, he went on to become the leading scorer in 1954–55 with 11 goals in 38 games. He was released under Tom Parker's management and went to play for Yarmouth Town, but was re-signed after the new Norwich board took over in February 1957. He went on to score 52 goals in 250 league and cup games after which he took up a coaching post with King's Lynn.

BRIBERY In November 1913, Birmingham full-back and captain Frank Womack was approached by a man who offered him 55 guineas (£57.75) to help fix the club's game against Grimsby Town at the end of the month, so that it would end in a draw. The Blues' captain reported the matter to the local police via the club's officials and the culprit was arrested and dealt with in the Assize Court. For the record, the Mariners won 2–1.

BRIDGES, BARRY A former England Schoolboy international, Barry Bridges joined Chelsea's ground-staff in the summer of 1956 and signed professional forms two years later. Following the departure of Jimmy Greaves to AC Milan, Bridges established himself in the Chelsea side and in April 1965 won the first of four full caps for England when he played in a 2–2 draw against Scotland at Wembley. His only goal for his country came the following month in a 1–1 draw with Yugoslavia. He went on to score 93 goals in 205 games for the Stamford Bridge club before leaving to join Birmingham City in May 1966 for a fee of £55,000. He played his first game for the Blues on the opening day of the 1966–67 season when two goals from former Chelsea team-mate Bert Murray gave City a 2–1 win at Wolves. He scored his first goal for the club four days later in a 5–4 win over Portsmouth at Fratton Park, ending the season with 18 goals in 52 league and cup games. In 1967–68, Bridges was the club's leading goalscorer with 29 goals in 50 games including a hat-trick in a 4–1 home win over Rotherham United. After just two games of the following season, Bridges, who had scored 47 goals in 104 games, left St Andrew's to join Queen's Park Rangers. He scored 35 goals in 82 games for the Loftus Road club, later playing for Millwall and Brighton before retiring in 1974.

BRIGGS, GEORGE George 'Nippy' Briggs joined the Blues from Midland League club Denaby United in December 1923 and made his début in a 2–0 home defeat at the hands of Nottingham Forest. However, it was midway through the 1924–25 season before he established himself in the Birmingham first team after which he was a regular for eight seasons. The scorer of a number of vital goals, he netted his first hat-trick for the club in March 1928 in a 4–1 home win over Sheffield United. In 1930–31 he was the club's leading scorer in the league with 15 goals and was instrumental in the Blues reaching that season's FA Cup final. He went on to score 107 goals in 324 league and cup games before leaving St Andrew's in the summer of 1933 and joining Plymouth Argyle. He ended his playing days at Home Park before taking up coaching.

BRIGGS, TOMMY Tommy Briggs was a butcher by trade and played junior football in the Doncaster area. During the war he served in the Royal Navy and, being stationed in Plymouth, he 'guested' for Argyle. In May 1947 he arrived on trial at Grimsby Town and scored 87 goals in 135 league appearances during the following four seasons. In 1949–50 he was the top marksman in the Football League with 36 goals and in January 1950 he was capped by England at 'B' international level. In December 1950 he joined Coventry City for a fee of £20,000 but within nine months he was on his way to St Andrew's in exchange for Don Dorman. He made a goalscoring début for the Blues in a 3–1 win at Everton and ended the season with 19 goals in 35 games as the St Andrew's club finished third in Division Two. He then became unsettled and after scoring 23 goals in 52 games, left to join Blackburn Rovers for £15,000. He was very popular with the Blackburn fans, topping 30 league goals in four successive seasons. In 1954–55 he was again the league's top scorer with 33 goals. Another personal triumph came in the match against Bristol Rovers when he scored seven goals in succession in an 8–3 win. He had scored 143 goals in 204 games for Rovers when he was allowed to return to Grimsby. A year later he moved to Ireland as player–manager at Glentoran before working for a radio and television firm in Grimsby.

BROADHURST, KEVIN Dewsbury-born defender Kevin Broadhurst had trials with both Bradford City and Manchester City before becoming an apprentice with the St Andrew's club in the summer of 1975. He made his league début for the Blues against Norwich City in February 1977, scoring one of Birmingham's goals in a 3–2 home win. The following month he signed full-time professional forms, though it was midway through the 1978–79 season before he won a regular first-team place. Though he was a member of the City side for the next six seasons, he missed a good number of games through injuries to his ankles and knees. When he was on the side, his impressive performances led to him winning selection for the England Under-21 side to play Holland in Alkmaar. Sadly for Broadhurst, an ice-bound pitch caused the game to be postponed and he was never selected again. After a constant battle against injuries, Broadhurst was forced to give up the game after scoring 10 goals in 173 league and cup games. He later returned to action with Midland Combination side Knowle North Star.

Kevin Broadhurst

BROCKLEBANK, BOB One of eight brothers, Bob Brocklebank was one of Finchley's most illustrious players before joining Aston Villa. His opportunities at Villa Park were limited, however, and he moved to play for Burnley. He scored 33 goals in 121 league games for the Clarets but scored many more during wartime football. After the war he became Chesterfield's manager and after establishing them in the Second Division, he joined Birmingham as a replacement for Harry Storer who had left the club six weeks earlier. Despite the Blues suffering relegation from Division One at the end of his first season at St Andrew's, Brocklebank was not overawed and in 1951, he took the club to the FA Cup semi-finals where they lost 2–1 to Blackpool in a replay. He brought a number of fine players to St Andrew's including Len Boyd, who was his first signing as Birmingham manager. In effect it was Brocklebank who put together the club's 1954–55 Second Division championship-winning side and the following season's FA Cup final team, even though he left the club in October 1954. He was on the staff of West Bromwich Albion when Hull City asked him to be their manager. He helped the Tigers win promotion to the Second Division before resigning to take over the reins at Bradford City. In his first season, City finished fifth in Division Four. They then had to apply for re-election and in 1963–64 were fifth again! Disillusioned by a poor start to the 1964–65 campaign, he resigned.

BROTHERS There have been a number of instances of brothers playing for Birmingham: there were three James brothers, for instance, who were involved in the founding of the Blues. The oldest was Fred who played left-back in the club's first-ever match against Holte Wanderers; the middle one was Arthur who represented the Birmingham FA XI on a number of occasions; and the youngest, Tommy, who had the shortest career. Also around at that time were the Edden brothers – Will, George and Tom. Goalkeeper Chris Charsley was the first player to be capped whilst a member of the Blues and his younger brother, Walter, made just three appearances for the club during the 1890–91 season in the Football Alliance. One of the club's pre-league stars was Will Devey who also captained the Blues. He scored six goals in a 12–0 win over Nottingham Forest and during his career with the club netted four hat-tricks. Ted Devey was a hard-working midfielder, whilst other brothers – Jack, Harry and Bob – all played for Aston Villa. Though Micky and Peter Bullock played for the Blues in the early 1960s, they only appeared in the same Birmingham side on one occasion – 17 April 1965, when the Blues lost 2–1 at Sunderland. The Latchford brothers Bob and Dave both made their Birmingham débuts in the 1968–69 season and, after playing in two games apiece, appeared in the same Blues' side together for the first of 90 occasions in a 2–1 win at Hull City. Scottish international Des Bremner made his name with Aston Villa before joining the Blues in September 1984. He made 195 appearances for the club before leaving to play for Walsall whilst his younger brother Kevin made four appearances on loan during the 1982–83 season.

BROWN, EDDIE A one-time theological student who studied in the Channel Islands before being evacuated during the war, Eddie Brown was one of the fastest strikers in the game at that time. He began his league career with his home-town club, Preston North End, and after making his début during the 1948–49 season, he top-scored for the club the following campaign with 12 goals in 24 games. In September 1950 he was exchanged for Southampton's Charlie Wayman and ended his first season at The Dell as the Saints' leading scorer with 20 goals in 36 games. He started the 1951–52 season in a similar vein and had scored 12 goals in 21 games (including a hat-trick in a 5–2 home win over Nottingham Forest) when he decided he wanted to leave the south coast club and asked for a transfer. Moving to Coventry City in March 1952, he continued to score on a regular basis, netting 50 goals in 85 league games. In October 1954 he left Highfield Road to join Birmingham City and made his début in a 2–0 home win over Swansea Town. That season the club won the Second Division Championship and Brown ended the campaign with 14 goals in 28 games including a hat-trick in a 9–1 home win over Liverpool. In 1955–56 Brown was the club's leading scorer with 28 league and cup goals, including a hat-trick in a 7–1 third round FA Cup win at Torquay United. He went on to score 90 goals for the Blues in 185 games before he left St Andrew's to join Leyton Orient in January 1959. Brown, who had scored 190 goals in 399 league games for his five clubs, then played non-league football for Scarborough, Stourbridge, Bedworth Town and Wigan Athletic.

BRUCE, STEVE Steve Bruce was introduced to league football by Gillingham and made his début at Blackpool in August 1979. He missed just six matches that season as a midfield player, but soon switched to a defensive role, becoming one of the Third Division's most outstanding players. Norwich City signed him for £125,000

Steve Bruce

in the summer of 1984 and, though the club were relegated at the end of his first season at Carrow Road, he won a League Cup winners' medal as Sunderland were beaten 1–0. The following season he helped the Canaries bounce back to the top flight as they won the Second Division Championship. He went on to play in 180 first-team games for Norwich until, after a seemingly interminable wrangle with the Canaries board, he joined Manchester United for £800,000 in December 1987. Despite breaking his nose and conceding a penalty on his début at Portsmouth, he soon settled in alongside Gary Pallister at the heart of the defence. He won an FA Cup winners' medal in 1990 and a European Cup Winners' Cup medal in 1991. Always dangerous at set pieces, he was the club's leading scorer in 1990–91 with 20 goals of which over half were penalties. He won a League Cup winners' medal in 1992 before being appointed team captain for the start of the newly formed Premier League in 1992–93. He then proceeded to lead United to three Premier League titles in the space of four years but, having scored 52 goals in 425 games, he nevertheless rejected the prospect of a lucrative testimonial at Old Trafford to join Birmingham City instead as club captain under new manager Trevor Francis. He made his début in the 1–0 home win over Crystal Palace on the opening day of the 1996–97 season and was soon an integral member of City's defence. His leadership qualities were always in evidence and though he fractured an eye socket in March 1997, forcing him to miss nine games, he was still voted runner-up in the club's Player of the Year award. He was inspirational in the heart of the Blues' defence in 1997–98 and won the Player of the Year award by a margin. Sadly, he left St Andrew's in the summer of 1998 after just 84 first-team appearances for the Blues to join Sheffield United as player–manager. In the summer of 1999 he left Bramall Lane to take charge of Huddersfield Town.

BURNS, KENNY Though he began his career with Glasgow Rangers, it was with Birmingham City that Kenny Burns first came into prominence. He joined the St Andrew's club as an apprentice in the summer of 1970 and signed professional forms the following year. His first game for the Blues was as a substitute in a 1–0 defeat at Hull City in September 1971, though it was 1973–74 before he established himself as a first-team regular at St Andrew's. During that season he scored 10 goals in 37 league games including a hat-trick in a 3–3 draw at Leicester City. In his last season with the club, 1976–77, Burns formed a formidable striking partnership with Trevor Francis and scored 19 goals in 36 games including four in a 5–1 home win over Derby County. Though he had more than his fair share of disciplinary problems,

Kenny Burns

he had scored 53 goals in 204 games for the Blues when Brian Clough signed him for Nottingham Forest in the summer of 1977. Playing solely as a defender, Burns was outstanding as Forest won the League Championship and League Cup in his first season with the club. He was selected as the Football Writers'

Association Player of the Year and went to Argentina with the Scotland World Cup squad. He won 12 caps during his stay at the City Ground and a total of 20 in his career. After winning a League Championship medal, League Cup winners' medal and two European Cup medals, the popular Scotsman was transferred to Leeds United after 196 appearances for the Reds. After Elland Road, he played for Derby County and Barnsley before playing non-league football with Sutton Town, Stafford Rangers and Heanor Town.

C

CALDERWOOD, JIMMY A fine utility player, Jimmy Calderwood joined Birmingham City from Glasgow Amateurs in the summer of 1971 and made his début in a 2–1 win at Stoke City in November 1972. Despite only appearing in 14 league games in his first two seasons at St Andrew's, he became an important member of the Blues' first-team squad and went on to score five goals in 159 games. Though he wore eight different numbered shirts for Birmingham, he preferred to play at right-back where his good positional play and strong tackling made him a popular player with the club's supporters. After losing his place to Terry Lees and finally Kevin Broadhurst, he went on loan to Cambridge United but declined a permanent move to the Abbey Stadium. Instead, he opted to play as a non-contract professional with Dutch side Sparta Rotterdam, later turning out for Willem II and Roda JC, both members of the Dutch League.

CAMKIN, BILL Bill Camkin was the club's honorary managing director throughout the Second World War, looking after team affairs and running the club in conjunction with Sam Richards. Camkin steered the Blues through the hostilities and, despite the bombing of St Andrew's by German planes and the fire which destroyed the Main Stand and many of his personal belongings, he kept the club going. His efforts on behalf of the Blues were greatly appreciated by both players and supporters. Sadly, during the 1952–53 season, he was dogged by ill-health which forced him to give up his position as a director.

CAMPBELL, ALAN The Arbroath-born midfielder began his Football League career with Charlton Athletic and in five seasons at The Valley, he made over 200 league and cup appearances before joining Birmingham City in October 1970 for a fee of

Jimmy Calderwood

£10,000. After making his début in a 5–2 defeat at Queen's Park Rangers, the Scottish Youth international won Under-23 honours and soon settled into one of the club's finest sides. Adept at finding space and a fine passer of the ball, Campbell was a distinctive figure on the field of play with his long dark hair and a shirt which always looked far too big for him! In 1971–72 he was one of three ever-presents as the Blues won promotion to the First Division and, over the next four seasons, he hardly missed a game. Early in the 1975–76 campaign he lost his place to Malcolm Page and, having scored 14 goals in 209 games, he joined Cardiff City for £20,000. In his first season at Ninian Park he helped the Bluebirds win promotion to the Second Division and had made

190 league and cup appearances in five years with the club when he left to join Carlisle United where injury forced him to leave league football.

CAPACITY The total capacity of St Andrew's in 1998–99 was 25,812.

CAPS The most capped player in the club's history is Malcolm Page who won 28 caps for Wales.

CAPS (ENGLAND) The first Birmingham City player to be capped by England was Chris Charsley when he played against Ireland in 1892–93. The most capped player is goalkeeper Harry Hibbs with 25 caps.

CAPS (NORTHERN IRELAND) The first Birmingham City player to be capped by Northern Ireland was John Brown when he played against Scotland in 1938–39. Only four City players have represented Northern Ireland at full international level – Bobby Brennan, John Brown, Ray Ferris and Jon McCarthy – and all have been capped three times.

CAPS (REPUBLIC OF IRELAND) The first Birmingham City player to be capped by the Republic of Ireland was James Higgins who played against Argentina in 1950–51. The most capped player is Don Givens with 14 caps.

CAPS (SCOTLAND) The first Birmingham City player to be capped by Scotland was Johnny Crosbie when he played against England in 1921–22. The most capped player is Archie Gemmill with 10 caps.

CAPS (WALES) The first Birmingham City player to be capped by Wales was Caesar Jenkyns when he played against England in 1891–92. The most capped player is Malcolm Page with 28 caps.

CAPTAINS Among the many players who have captained the club are Billy Edmunds, the Blues' first official captain, appointed in 1877, who played in the club's first-ever game in 1875. Caesar Jenkyns was a born leader and captained every team that he played for, leading the Blues to the Second Division Championship in

1892–93 in what was the club's first season in the Football League. Alex McClure captained the club's reserve side to victory in three competitions before winning a first-team place and skippering the club to the Second Division Championship in 1920–21. Ned Barkas, who won two League Championship medals with Huddersfield Town, captained the Blues to their first FA Cup final appearance in 1931 whilst Fred Harris led the club to the Second Diviison title in 1947–48. Len Boyd, who began his career with Plymouth Argyle, skippered the Blues to the Second Division Championship in 1954–55 and to a second FA Cup final appearance the following season. Other captains in recent years have included Malcolm Page who also skippered Wales, Gary Pendrey who led the Blues' youth team to the FA Cup final in 1967 and Steve Bruce who joined the club from Manchester United.

CARROLL, TOMMY Dublin-born full-back Tommy Carroll began his career with Shelbourne where he won an Irish League Championship medal in 1962. He later starred in both the European Cup and European Cup Winners' Cup for the Irish club and appeared in every outfield position in his time with them. After a spell of playing non-league football for Cambridge City, he joined Ipswich Town in the summer of 1966 but had to wait until March 1967 before making his début at Hull City. Capped 17 times by the Republic of Ireland, Carroll was an important member of the Suffolk club's 1967–68 Second Division Championship-winning side. In 1969–70, Carroll was the club's only ever-present but soon became unsettled and in October 1971, after appearing in 126 first-team games, he left Portman Road to join Birmingham City. His first game for the Blues was in a 1–1 draw at Burnley after which he played in all but one of the remaining 27 games as the club won promotion to the First Division. Carroll started the 1972–73 season in the top flight as the Blues' first choice right-back but, sadly, after just 47 first-team appearances, injury forced him to quit competitive football.

CENTENARY MATCH Glasgow Celtic visited St Andrew's for the Centenary Match on 25 November 1975. A crowd of 14,670 saw Peter Withe score the only goal of the game to bring the Blues a deserved victory.

CENTURIES Three individual players have scored 100 or more league goals for Birmingham City. Joe Bradford is the greatest goalscorer with 249 strikes in his St Andrew's career (1920–1935). Other centurions are Trevor Francis (118) and Peter Murphy (107). Two goalkeepers, Dan Tremelling and Gil Merrick, hold the club record for the most consecutive league appearances – 126. Another goalkeeper, Arthur Robinson, is the only other City player to have made over 100 consecutive league appearances during his career, playing in 107 matches.

CHAMPIONSHIPS Birmingham have won a divisional championship on five occasions. The Second Division of the Football League was formed in 1892 and the Blues, along with other members of the Football Alliance, were elected members. In their first season, they scored 90 goals in 22 games and carried off the title in style. Victories included Walsall Town Swifts (Home 12–0) and Grimsby Town (Home 8–3) whilst the club scored six goals on four occasions. Yet, despite winning the first-ever Second Division Championship, the club were unable to claim a First Division place after losing to Newton Heath in the Test matches – a forerunner of today's play-offs. The Blues won the Second Division Championship again in 1920–21, scoring 79 goals, conceding 38 and totalling 58 points. The only ever-present was Johnny Crosbie and it was he who was instrumental in guiding the club to the title. When Birmingham won the Second Division Championship for a third time in 1947–48, they established a new club defensive record, conceding just 24 goals whilst only losing five of their 42 matches. The club's performance in winning the Second Division Championship in 1954–55 was all the more remarkable considering that at one stage they occupied their lowest league position since the Second World War. During successive home games Port Vale were beaten 7–2 and Liverpool 9–1 but, towards the end of the season, they were still nine points adrift of the leaders. However, they had four games in hand and eventually went into the last game of the season needing to win at Doncaster Rovers to lift the championship. In a truly brilliant performance, the Blues won 5–1 to take the title by 0.297 of a goal. The club last won a divisional championship in 1994–95 when they won the Second Division title, finishing four points ahead of runners-up

Brentford. During the course of the season, the club embarked on an unbeaten run of 20 matches which included a 7–1 home win over Blackpool.

CHARSLEY, CHRIS Goalkeeper Chris Charsley played his early football with Stafford FC and Stafford Rangers, but in 1882 he joined the Birmingham police force. He remained an amateur throughout his playing career which revolved around his work as a police officer. In 1885–86 after 'guesting' for Aston Villa, he joined the Blues and made his début against Mitchell St George's in an FA Cup tie. By this time Charsley had been appointed to the position of chief inspector, but he continued to keep goal for the Blues until 1891 when he signed for West Bromwich Albion. Within weeks he was back at Muntz Street and in 1892–93 he helped the club win the Second Division Championship. That season also saw him win his one full cap for England when he played in a 6–1 win over Ireland at Birmingham. He left the game at the end of the 1893–94 season and was later appointed chief constable of Coventry, a position he held for 19 years.

CLARIDGE, STEVE Steve Claridge began his league career with Bournemouth whom he joined from Fareham Town in November 1984. After just a handful of games for the Cherries, he returned to non-league football with Weymouth. His goalscoring performances for the Dorset club led to Crystal Palace signing him in October 1988 but, having failed to make the grade with the Selhurst Park club, he joined Aldershot. He had scored 22 goals in 76 games for the club when Cambridge United paid £75,000 for his services in February 1990. The bustling striker continued to find the net, scoring 31 times in 95 first-team outings before Luton Town splashed out £160,000 to take him to Kenilworth Road in the summer of 1992. His stay was brief and within four months he was back with Cambridge who had to pay an extra £35,000 more than they had received in order to take him to the Abbey Stadium. He took his tally for the East Anglian club to 52 goals in 159 games before Birmingham City paid £350,000 for him in January 1994. He made his début for the Blues in a 2–1 defeat at Notts County and, though he scored five goals in five games at the end of the season, it wasn't enough to prevent the club from being relegated to the Second Division. In

THE ST ANDREW'S ENCYCLOPEDIA

Steve Claridge

1994–95, when the Blues won the Second Division Championship, Claridge was the top scorer with 20 goals in 42 games but in March 1996, after scoring 42 goals in 120 league and cup games, he was sold to Leicester City for £1.2 million. After helping the Foxes reach the play-off final at Wembley, he scored a 90th-minute goal there to help beat Crystal Palace 1–0 and take the Filbert Street club into the Premiership. Certainly not out of place in the top flight, he had scored 21 goals in 79 games before joining Wolves for £400,000 in March 1998. He is now playing for Portsmouth with whom he got a loan spell in 1997–98.

CLARKE, WAYNE Much-travelled striker Wayne Clarke began his Football League career with Wolverhampton Wanderers, though after making his début at Ipswich on the last day of the 1977–78 season, it took him a few seasons to establish himself. In fact, it wasn't until 1982–83 when the Molineux club won promotion from the Second Division that he showed his goalscoring talents, netting 12 times in 39 games. He had scored 33 goals in 170 games for Wolves when the Blues paid £80,000 for his services in the summer of 1984. He made his début in a 1–0 win at Oldham Athletic on the opening day of the 1984–85 season, ending the campaign as the club's top scorer with 17 goals in 40 league games as the Blues won promotion. After a disappointing 1985–86 season in which City were relegated, he rediscovered his shooting boots and had scored 18 goals in 28 games when Everton paid £300,000 to take him to Goodison Park. Clarke, who had scored 43 goals in 105 games for Birmingham, helped the Merseyside club win the League Championship for the second time in three years as well as scoring the only goal in the 1987 Charity Shield win over Coventry City. A member of a famous footballing family, he later played for Manchester City and Walsall before returning to Wolves on loan. He ended his first-class career with Shrewsbury Town, whom he helped win the Third Division Championship in 1993–94.

CLEAN SHEET This is the colloquial expression used to describe a goalkeeper's performance when he does not concede a goal. When the Blues won the Second Division Championship in 1947–48, Gil Merrick had 22 clean sheets in 36 league appearances. In recent years, Ian Bennett had 21 clean sheets in 45 games during the club's 1997–98 season.

COLOURS The club's colours are blue shirts, white shorts, blue and white hooped stockings, whilst their change colours are white shirts with black stripes and black shorts.

CONSECUTIVE HOME GAMES The Blues have played an extraordinarily intense sequence of seven home games in succession in just 55 days (2 February–28 March 1895).

Date	Opponents	Competition	Score
02.02.1895	West Bromwich Albion	FA Cup Round 1	1–2
09.02.1895	Sunderland	Division One	1–1
23.02.1895	West Bromwich Albion	Division One	1–2
02.03.1895	Blackburn Rovers	Division One	1–1
16.03.1895	Derby County	Division One	3–5
23.03.1895	Burnley	Division One	1–0
28.03.1895	Sheffield Wednesday	Division One	0–0

CONSECUTIVE SCORING – LONGEST SEQUENCE Trevor Francis holds the club record for consecutive scoring on account of his eight consecutive league games in which he scored 13 goals. His first came in the 3–1 home win over Millwall on 6 February 1971 and the last when he scored the opening goal in a 2–0 win over Cardiff City at St Andrew's on 27 March 1971.

COOPER, TERRY Terry Cooper won a reputation as a fine, attacking left-back with Leeds United. Though his goals were relatively rare, he scored against Arsenal in the 1968 League Cup final to give Leeds their first major trophy. Two years later he won the first of 20 full caps for England and played in the 1970 World Cup. Cooper went on to make 350 appearances for the Elland Road club before joining Middlesbrough in March 1975. He later had a spell at Bristol City before becoming player-coach at Bristol Rovers. In his first season at Eastville, the club were relegated and the Main Stand burnt down. Dismissed in 1981, he played briefly for Doncaster Rovers before joining Bristol City as player-manager. He took them to promotion to Division Three and to the Freight Rover Trophy final in 1986 and 1987. He later joined the board, thus becoming the first player–manager director since Vivian Woodward at the turn of the century. Sacked in March 1988, he managed Exeter City to the Fourth Division title in

Tony Coton

1989–90 before taking charge of the Blues in August 1991. At the end of his first season at St Andrew's he led the Blues to promotion as runners-up in the Third Division. In 1992–93 the club were fortunate not to be relegated. They had new owners and an injection of cash for the City manager to use on the transfer market but still the Blues struggled – they only saved themselves with a win over Charlton Athletic on the last day. Rejoining Exeter City as manager in January 1994, ill-health forced his resignation but in the summer of 1996, he joined Southampton's coaching staff.

COTON, TONY Goalkeeper Tony Coton joined the Blues from Mile Oak Rovers of Tamworth in October 1978 and made a sensational start to his Football League career on his début as City faced Sunderland at St Andrew's on 27 December 1978. With less than a minute gone, the visitors were awarded a penalty but Coton saved it. He became a regular in the Birmingham side early in 1982–83 after contesting the keeper's jersey with both Jeff Wealands and Jim Blyth. He had appeared in 114 league and cup games when he left St Andrew's to join First Division Watford. He soon became a big favourite at Vicarage Road and was voted Player of the Year on three separate occasions. However, he was transferred to Manchester City in the summer of 1990 when the club, which needed money desperately, was forced to sell one of its major assets. Coton had played in 291 games for the Hornets and cost the Maine Road club £1 million. In his first season a series of fine displays took him into the England reckoning, yet his only international honour was as a substitute in an England 'B' match in 1991–92. He appeared in 194 games for the Maine Road club before moving across the city to join Manchester United. Having failed to break into the club's first team, he left to join Sunderland in July 1996. After only 10 appearances in the Premier League he was involved in an accidental collision with Southampton striker Egil Ostenstad and fractured his leg in five places.

CRICKETERS There have been a number of Birmingham players who were also cricketers of real note. Fred Wheldon, who helped the Blues win the Second Division Championship in 1892–93 and promotion the following year, came to the fore with Aston Villa where he won international recognition, three League Championship medals and an FA Cup winners' medal. He also played cricket for Worcestershire where he was a good middle-order batsman and wicket-keeper. He scored 4,938 runs at 22.25 and a top score of 112 against Somerset in 1903. Alonzo Drake spent just one season with the Blues, appearing in 11 games at inside-forward in 1907–08 and scoring two goals, one of which was on his home début in a 2–1 win over Sheffield Wednesday. In addition, he scored 4,804 runs at 21.73 and took 482 wickets at 17.89 runs apiece for Yorkshire. In 1913 he did the 'double', scoring 1,029 runs and taking 115 wickets. Drake also achieved the hat-trick on two occasions. His best bowling figures were 10 for 35 against Somerset in 1914. John Higgins, who made just one appearance for Birmingham, scored 3,837 runs for Worcestershire at an average of 19.78 and took 28 wickets at 47.82 runs each. Arthur Foster had one match for Warwickshire in 1914 when he kept wicket, taking two catches and scoring one run. Winger Bill Harvey, who played in 78 games for the Blues in the 1920s, also played one game for Warwickshire in 1927, scoring 24 runs. Jimmy Windridge, who scored five goals against Glossop, scored 161 runs and took one for 13 in seven games for Warwickshire. Arthur Mounteney scored 30 goals in 97 games for the Blues, and played for Leicestershire for 13 seasons, scoring 5,306 runs at 20.81 and capturing 17 wickets at 29.65 runs apiece. Birmingham manager Harry Storer played first-class cricket for Derbyshire and in 16 seasons with the county scored 13,513 runs at 27.63. He top scored with 232 against Essex at Derby in 1933 and took 232 wickets at 32.43 runs each. Australian-born Frank Mitchell had wanted to play cricket for the country of his birth, but after coming to England with his parents, joined the Warwickshire CCC ground staff. He made only a few appearances at county level, scoring 224 runs at 8.30 and taking 22 wickets at 38.91. He won a Second Division Championship medal for the Blues in 1947–48 before later playing for Chelsea and Watford. Mike Hellawell had two matches for Warwickshire in 1962, scoring 59 runs and taking six wickets for 114 runs.

CRINIGAN, JIMMY The brother of Celtic and Scottish international Willie Crinigan, Jimmy began his playing career with Douglas Water Thistle. Though he had trials with Sunderland, Dunfermline Athletic and Falkirk, he failed to impress and returned to play for Thistle before Birmingham signed him on professional terms in the summer of 1923. He made his début for the St Andrew's club in a 1–1 draw at Sunderland on 15 September 1923 and over the next nine seasons was a first-team regular. After playing his first couple of games at inside-forward, he reverted to playing centre-half though he did appear in all three half-back positions. Crinigan also fancied himself as a goalkeeper and when the Blues were on tour, he replaced the injured Harry Hibbs. A member of the Blues' FA Cup final side of 1931, he scored 12 goals in 284 league and cup games before leaving to join Boston United as player–manager in 1934.

CROSBIE, JOHNNY Scottish international Johnny Crosbie began his career with his home-town team, Glenbuck Cherrypickers, before playing for Muirkirk Athletic and Ayr United. Known to the fans as 'Peerless', he joined the Blues in the summer of 1920 and made his début in the opening game of the 1920–21 season in a 3–0 defeat at South Shields. In fact, Crosbie was the club's only ever-present that campaign, and scored 14 goals as the Blues won the Second Division Championship. In the top flight, Crosbie and Bradford were joint-top scorers with 10 goals but it was as a provider rather than a taker of chances that the Scotsman was to make his name. Crosbie went on to score 72 goals in 432 league and cup games for Birmingham and in his penultimate season with the club, appeared in their 2–1 FA Cup final defeat against West Bromwich Albion in 1931. After leaving St Andrew's, Crosbie had a brief spell with Chesterfield before becoming player–manager of Stourbridge. He later coached in Sweden before severing all connections with the game.

CROWD TROUBLE When Birmingham entertained Leeds United on 11 May 1985, 96 police were hurt and one innocent fan, who was attending his first proper game, was killed when a wall collapsed in the corner between the Tilton Road End and the Main Stand. St Andrew's also witnessed one of the worst disturbances at a Football League ground for a good number of years when the Third Division match between Birmingham City and Stoke City on 29 February 1992 was halted by a pitch invasion. The incident was sparked by Stoke scoring a late controversial equaliser. When Birmingham then had a shot cleared off the line, hundreds of City fans swarmed on to the pitch and one of them attacked the referee Roger Wiseman. The Birmingham chairman, Samesh Kumar, appealed to the fans to calm down and when he was ignored, it was announced that the match would not continue. But 20 minutes later, when police had cleared the ground, the remaining 35 seconds of the game were played. The club's cause was not helped by Kumar who said that the referee had made some scandalous decisions. His outburst led to him being charged with misconduct by the FA. The club were fined £50,000 and ordered to play two matches behind closed doors.

CULLIS, STAN Stan Cullis was appointed captain of Wolverhampton Wanderers before he was 20 and in later years captained his country. With England he won 12 full caps plus a further 20 in wartime internationals when he formed a brilliant half-back line with Joe Mercer and Cliff Britton. He appeared for Wolves in the 1939 FA Cup final and, though he lost seven seasons to the Second World War, he was a first-team regular when league football resumed in 1946–47. He retired from playing at the end of that season, having appeared in 171 league and cup games for the club. He then became assistant-manager to Ted Vizard at Molineux before being appointed manager in June 1948. Under his guidance, Wolves won three League titles in 1953–54, 1957–58 and 1958–59. They also lifted the FA Cup in 1949 and 1960, the FA Charity Shield, the FA Youth Cup and in the late 1950s they entered European competition. Later, when things began to go wrong and Wolves were near the foot of the First Division, Cullis was sacked. After a year out of the game he was appointed manager of Birmingham City in December 1965. The Blues hoped that his experience would guide them back to the First Division but, despite an improvement in performances, it wasn't to be. He did lead the Blues to the semi-finals of both the FA and League Cups but the highest the club finished in the league before his departure in March 1970 was fourth in Division Two in 1967–68.

CURBISHLEY, ALAN A midfield playmaker who played for England Schoolboys and England Youth, Alan Curbishley was a member of the West Ham United side which reached the FA Youth Cup final in 1975. He made his first-team début for the Hammers in a 1–0 home defeat by Chelsea in March 1975 and, over the next four seasons, played in 96 league and cup games for the club. However, after failing to beat off the competition of Brooking and Devonshire, he left Upton Park to join Birmingham City. His first game for the Blues came in a 4–3 home defeat by

Alan Curbishley

Fulham on the opening day of the 1979–80 season, a campaign in which he appeared in every game for the club as they won promotion to the First Division. Curbishley played in the majority of City's games over the next five seasons but in March 1983, after scoring 21 goals in 187 games, he signed for neighbours Aston Villa. He later appeared in 116 league games for Brighton, sandwiched between two spells with Charlton Athletic where he is now manager, having taken the Addicks into the Premier League.

CURTIS, ERNIE A former Cardiff and Welsh Schoolboy footballer, he worked as an electrician whilst continuing to play amateur football. During the 1925–26 season, Cardiff City gave him the opportunity to show what he could do as an amateur trialist. After winning an amateur cap, he was offered full-time terms and made his début in a 2–0 defeat against Manchester United. He held his place for most of the season as the Bluebirds advanced to the FA Cup final against Arsenal. He was, at that time, the youngest player ever to appear in a Cup final, aged only 19 years. A few weeks later he added a Welsh Cup winners' medal to his collection when City beat Rhyl 2–0 to round off a fairy-tale campaign. In October 1927 he won his first Welsh cap against Scotland at Wrexham and scored in a 2–2 draw. In March 1928 he joined Birmingham for £3,000 and made his début in a 4–1 home win over Sheffield United. Playing most of his games for the St Andrew's club at outside-left, he was a member of the Blues' side beaten 2–1 by West Bromwich Albion in the 1931 FA Cup final. During that cup run, Curtis scored six goals and – including league games – netted 14 in 47 appearances. He had scored 53 goals in 182 games when he left to return to Ninian Park but his stay was short-lived due to his involvment in a dispute over the amount of wages he had been promised. He then joined Coventry where he also had a spell as player–coach before returning home at the outbreak of the Second World War. He joined the Royal Artillery but was captured by the Japanese and made a prisoner of war from 1941 to the end of the hostilities. On his return to Britain, he joined Cardiff for a third spell, this time as the club's reserve trainer, a post he held until he left the game in the early 1960s.

D

DALE, DICKIE Half-back Dickie Dale was playing as an amateur centre-half for West Hartlepool prior to his move to Birmingham in the summer of 1922. He made his début in the fourth game of the 1922–23 season in a goalless draw at Newcastle United and kept his place in the side for the next five seasons. Whilst with the Blues, Dale represented the Staffordshire County FA against the FA XI at Molineux and appeared in 151 first-team games before leaving to join West Bromwich Albion in November 1928. At the Hawthorns he acted as understudy to Bill Richardson but after just a handful of games, he was transferred to Tranmere Rovers where he made just 10 appearances for the Prenton Park club. He then played non-league football for Crook Town before a long-term injury forced his retirement.

DEARSON, DON The son of a Welsh miner, Don Dearson joined Birmingham from Barry Town in April 1934 and made his début in a 4–0 home defeat by Huddersfield Town in December 1934. In his first two seasons with the club, Dearson only featured in 10 league games but in 1936–37, after switching from inside-forward to wing-half, he established himself as a first-team regular. In fact, he had only appeared in a handful of games at right-half when he won the first of three caps for Wales, playing against Scotland in 1939. During the Second World War he 'guested' for a number of clubs including West Bromwich Albion, and appeared in 15 unofficial internationals for Wales. In 1945–46 he helped the Blues win the League (South) Championship, and when league football resumed in 1946–47, he was still a member of the club's first team. He had scored 17 goals in 137 league and cup games when in February 1947 he moved to Coventry City. After netting 11 goals in 88 games for the Sky Blues he joined Walsall until he left to play non-league football for Nuneaton Borough.

DEATH Jeff Hall died of polio a fortnight after having been taken ill in March 1959. The publicity surrounding the death of the 29-year-old left-back, who had never lost a game while playing for England, was instrumental in persuading the public to participate in a mass inoculation scheme to combat the disease.

DÉBUTS The only Blues player to score a hat-trick on his début is Peter Murphy who netted three goals in the 5–0 win over Doncaster Rovers at Belle Vue on 19 January 1952. England international centre-half Trevor Smith put through his own goal on his début in a 4–2 win at Derby County in October 1953. Welsh international goalkeeper Gary Sprake saved a penalty on his Birmingham début in a 1–0 defeat at Arsenal in October 1973 but in his next game he scored an own goal! When Birmingham City goalkeeper Tony Coton first touched the ball on his début, it was to save a penalty after 85 seconds. On 27 December 1980 he had been called into the Blues' side against Sunderland in a Division One match and stopped John Hawley's shot. For the record, Birmingham won 3–2. Paul Hart broke his leg on his Birmingham début against Plymouth Argyle in December 1986 as he collided with team-mate Tommy Williams. Sadly, it was his only appearance for the club.

DEFEATS – FEWEST Though the club lost only three games in winning the Second Division Championship in 1892–93 – their first season in the Football League – it was from a 22-match programme. The club's fewest defeats from a 42-match season are five in seasons 1947–48, when they won the Second Division, and 1971–72 when the Blues were runners-up in the same division.

DEFEATS – MOST A total of 29 defeats suffered during the 1985–86 season is the worst in the club's history. Not surprisingly, the club finished 21st in the First Division and were relegated.

DEFEATS – WORST Birmingham City's record defeat is 9–1, inflicted on them by both Blackburn Rovers in 1894–95 and Sheffield Wednesday in 1930–31. The club also lost a Football Alliance game by that scoreline when they were beaten by Newton Heath on the final day of the 1889–90 season. Birmingham's worst home defeat is 7–1, courtesy of Burnley in 1925–26 and West Bromwich Albion in 1959–60.

DEFENSIVE RECORD Birmingham's best defensive record was established in 1900–01 and then equalled in 1947–48. They conceded just 24 goals in each of those seasons but in 1900–01 they played just 34 games to finish runners-up in the Second Division. Their achievement in 1947–48 was from a 42-match programme as they won the Second Division Championship. Birmingham's worst defensive record was in 1964–65 when they conceded 96 goals to finish bottom of the First Division and be relegated.

DENNIS, MARK Mark Dennis broke into the Birmingham City side in 1978–79, making his début in a 4–0 defeat at Norwich City. The Streatham-born youngster made an immediate impact, not only for his immense talent but also for having a fiery temperament. His five seasons at St Andrew's were consequently stormy and, in November 1983, after making 145 first-team appearances for the Blues, he was sold to Southampton for £30,000. Whilst with Birmingham he won England Youth and Under-21 honours and his only goal for the club came in a 3–1 defeat at Ipswich in March 1983. At Southampton, the Saints' fans saw the two sides of Dennis – a skilful left-back who should have been challenging for England honours had it not been for his temper. He left The Dell after a series of clashes with manager Chris Nicholl and joined Queen's Park Rangers. During his first season at Loftus Road he was given a record 53 days' suspension by the FA after being sent off for the 11th time in his career. In the summer of 1989 he left to join Crystal Palace where he ended his league career.

DERBIES The rivalry between Birmingham City and Aston Villa has become an established part of the Football League scene. Aston Villa were founded in 1874 when cricketing enthusiasts of Villa Cross Wesleyan Chapel, Aston, decided to form a football club. Of the 96 league meetings between them, the Blues have won 32 and Villa 39. They have drawn 25. Birmingham have completed the double – that is, they have won both league games in a season – on five occasions, Villa eight times. The two clubs first met in the Football League at Perry Barr on the opening day of the 1894–95 season. Villa won 2–1 with Hands scoring for the Blues. The

Mark Dennis

following season, Villa completed their first double, winning 7–3 at home and 4–1 away. It was 1905–06 before the Blues got the better of Villa in a league match, winning 2–0 at Muntz Street with goals from Jones and Mounteney. In fact, the Blues won the return at Villa Park 3–1 to complete their first double. The games were usually hard fought and on 24 March 1923, Billy Walker converted two penalties awarded them due to the robust tackling of the visitors! During the 1963–64 season, former Villa full-back Stan Lynn scored from the penalty-spot against his former club in both games as the Blues won 3–0 at Villa Park on 30 March 1964 and drew 3–3 at St Andrew's the following day. In 1967–68, Barry Bridges scored two goals in each match as the Blues completed the double, winning 2–1 at home and 4–2 at Villa Park. The Blues' biggest victory over their rivals came on 21 September 1968 when they won 4–0 at St Andrew's with goals from Vowden, Greenhoff, Vincent and Summerill. The last time the clubs met in the league was at St Andrew's on 12 December 1987 when two Garry Thompson goals gave Villa a 2–1 win.

DEVEY, WILL Will Devey played for Clarendon Montrose and Wellington before joining Aston Villa as an amateur. In 1885 he joined the Blues as a professional alongside his brother Ted. The other members of the footballing family – Jack, Harry and Bob – all joined Aston Villa. In 1888, Will Devey was appointed the club captain, and over the next few seasons he certainly led by example. He scored four goals in a 9–0 FA Cup win over Burton Wanderers and was the club's top scorer in their first two seasons in the Football Alliance. In 1889–90 he scored six goals in the Blues' 12–0 win over Nottingham Forest and netted a hat-trick in a 4–0 FA Cup win over Walsall Town Swifts. The following season he netted a hat-trick against Crewe Alexandra in a 4–3 home win. After leaving the Blues, he played for Mitchell St George's before spending two years with Aston Villa. He later played for Walsall (in two spells), Burton Wanderers and Darlaston before being called upon to help the Blues out during a crisis in 1898–99. On his Football League début he scored Birmingham's goal in a 1–1 draw at Blackpool but after just one appearance at league level, he left to concentrate on his business in Birmingham.

DICKS, JULIAN The fierce-tackling left-back first came into League football with Birmingham City and made his début as a substitute in a 2–0 defeat at Chelsea in August 1985. Though the club were relegated in 1985–86, Dicks established himself as a first-team regular towards the end of the campaign and over the next two seasons appeared in 101 games before the shock announcement of his being sold to West Ham United for £300,000 in March 1988. At the end of that season he was selected

Julian Dicks

for the England Under-21 squad to compete in the annual summer tournament in the south of France. He was voted Hammer of the Year in 1989–90 and though he missed much of the following season with a serious knee injury, he returned to first-team action in December 1991, scoring from the penalty-spot in a 1–1 draw against Sheffield United. In 1992–93, despite being sent off three times, he scored 11 vital goals in 34 league matches as the Hammers returned to the top flight. In September 1993, with the Upton Park club languishing near the foot of the Premier League, he moved to Liverpool. Despite being sidelined by another knee injury, he still failed to win over the fans and in October 1994, the man they call 'The Terminator' returned to Upton Park. His consistency had no lack of backers wanting the 'bad boy' of football to be called up into the England squad. Sadly, the gifted defender has been plagued in recent seasons by injuries.

DILLON, KEVIN Sunderland-born Kevin Dillon began his Football League career with Birmingham City where much of his time at St Andrew's was spent at left-wing. It was from here that he scored some memorable goals, either with a curling shot or after a mazy dribble. He made his début for the Blues in a 1–1 home draw against Leicester City in November 1977 but it wasn't until 1978–79 that he established himself in the first team. One of the club's most influential players during their promotion-winning season of 1979–80, Dillon, who was capped by England at Youth and Under-21 levels, went on to appear in 212 games for the St Andrew's club before joining Portsmouth in March 1983 for a fee of £140,000. The fact that Dillon had a suspect temperament and was often in trouble with referees for back-chatting did not deter Pompey. Playing in the last 11 games of the 1983–84 season, he helped the club win promotion to the Second Division. He made 249 league and cup appearances for the Fratton Park club before returning to his native north-east to play for Newcastle United. He later joined Reading where he ended his career.

DISMISSALS Some of the club's earliest players were tough characters and were given their marching orders on a number of occasions. Percy Barton and Caesar Jenkyns, who captained the Blues to the Second Division Championship in 1892–93, were each sent off four times during their careers. Jenkyns, like Malcolm Beard, was sent off on his final appearance for the club. Gary Pendrey was sent off twice in his testimonial year and was charged with bringing the game into disrepute! Perhaps one of the most unusual dismissals befell Alex McClure in the match against Real Madrid in Spain. He was sent off for telling his own goalkeeper where to stand after a penalty had been awarded for

THE ST ANDREW'S ENCYCLOPEDIA

Kevin Dillon

hand-ball against Jack Jones who had his dentures smashed whilst trying to protect his face. The Spanish club's officials knew that there had been no deliberate offence and the referee made a written apology through the newspapers!

Louie Donowa

DONOWA, LOUIE Winger Louie Donowa was a member of the Norwich City FA Youth Cup-winning team of 1983 and scored on his full league début for the Canaries against Manchester United in October 1983. He collected a League Cup winners' medal in 1985, a season in which his excellent wing play won him three England Under-21 caps. After a loan spell at Stoke City, he spent three years on the Continent before returning to play for his home-town club Ipswich Town. A season at Bristol City was followed in August 1991 by a £60,000 move to Birmingham City. He made his début in a 1–0 home win over Darlington and went on to play in 26 games as the Blues won promotion from the old Division Three as runners-up to Brentford. Following a loan spell at Burnley, he returned to St Andrew's and immediately won back his first-team place in City's First Division side. Relegation in 1994 was followed by immediate promotion in 1995 – Donowa was on the Birmingham side which won the championship of the new Second Division. It was a double celebration, with the Blues also winning the Auto Windscreen Shield after beating Carlisle United by the only goal of the game in a sudden-death extra-time.

He went on to score 21 goals in 154 games for the Blues before going on for a spell with Peterborough United. He later joined Walsall where, after just seven games of the 1997–98 season, he was released.

DOUGALL, NEIL Falkirk-born Neil Dougall came from a footballing family: his father William played for Falkirk and Bury, and his nephew James was with Preston North End, Carlisle United and Halifax Town. Dougall joined Burnley and in March 1940 signed professional forms. He was in the RAF during the hostilities and 'guested' for both Coventry City and Walsall but in 1945 he joined the Blues. At the end of his first season with the St Andrew's club, he won a Football League (South) Championship medal, scoring 10 goals in 38 games, and helped the club reach the semi-final of the FA Cup. In 1946 he won a full cap for Scotland against Wales at Wrexham and in 1947–48 won a Second Division Championship medal. One of the club's most versatile forwards, he scored 18 goals in 108 league and cup games before joining Plymouth Argyle in March 1949 for a fee of £13,000. In ten seasons at Home Park, Dougall played in every outfield position except outside-left, scoring 26 goals in 289 league and cup games and winning two Third Division Championship medals. After becoming the club's trainer, he became the Pilgrims' manager but left after the club conceded five goals in each of three consecutive matches.

DRAWS Birmingham played their greatest number of drawn league matches in a single season in 1937–38 and 1971–72 when 18 of their matches ended all square. Their fewest number was in seasons 1895–96, 1897–98 and 1926–27 when only four of their matches were drawn. The club's highest scoring draw is 5–5, a scoreline achieved in two home matches, against Blackburn Rovers in 1964–65 and Derby County in 1965–66.

DUCKHOUSE, TED Centre-half Ted Duckhouse was originally a centre-forward when he joined Birmingham as a professional in 1938 after a season as an amateur with West Bromwich Albion. He scored on his début for the Blues in a 4–4 draw at Charlton Athletic on 1 October 1938 and netted another goal in his four league appearances that season. He played in a number of games for the Blues during the Second World War and in 1945–46 won a League South medal. He also played in all ten FA Cup games that season but, sadly, broke his leg in extra-time of the club's semi-final replay against Derby County. At the time Duckhouse was stretchered off the game was goalless, but the 10-man St Andrew's side went on to lose 4–0. In 1947–48, Duckhouse was an important member of the Birmingham side that won the Second Division Championship. He appeared in 36 games and was instrumental in the club conceding only 24 goals in the season – 18 in the games in which he played. He had appeared in 187 league and cup games for the Blues when in August 1950 he was allowed to sign for Northampton Town. He appeared in 68 league games for the Cobblers before ending his playing career with non-league Rushden Town.

E

EARLY GROUNDS The club's first ground was on wasteland next to Arthur Street, close to St Andrew's, but at the start of the 1876–77 season they moved to Ladypool Road, Sparkbrook, where they rented an enclosed pitch. However, the club moved back to Small Heath later on and rented a field behind Muntz Street for £5 a year. The club were to play at Muntz Street for 29 years.

EDMUNDS, BILLY Billy Edmunds played in the club's first-ever match in 1875 and in 1877–78 was appointed as the Blues' first captain. Positioned at half-back, he led the team as they played 22 games without defeat, appearing in every game. In 1879 he was credited with having scored a hat-trick in the space of five minutes! The match was a friendly against Nechells and Edmunds scored two goals for the Blues and then an own goal in the dying seconds to give Nechells a 4–3 victory. In 1882 he was appointed as the club's first honorary secretary and, though he handed over to Walter Hart two years later, he continued to work for the club behind the scenes on a part-time basis. On leaving the game, (and he never played a League or a Cup match for the Blues) he became a very successful businessman.

EDWARDS, GEORGE One of football's outstanding wingers of the 1940s, George Edwards began his career as an amateur with Swansea and made his first-team début towards the end of the 1938–39 season. Before the outbreak of the Second World War, he won a Welsh Amateur cap against England. During the war years he continued to play for Swansea whilst studying for a degree at Swansea University, but when he was called up for the RAF he was stationed in the Midlands and 'guested' for Coventry City. In 1945–46 he played for Wales in the Victory Internationals and in October 1946 he won his first full cap against Scotland. By now, Edwards was a Birmingham player, having helped them win the League South title in 1945–46 and having made his league debut in a 2–1 win at Spurs on the opening day of the 1946–47 season. He helped the Blues win the Second Division Championship in 1947–48 and, though he only scored nine goals in 99 games for the Blues, they were usually very crucial strikes. In December 1948 he joined Cardiff City for £12,000 and was a member of the Bluebirds' team that won promotion to the First Division in 1951–52. He went on to score 34 goals in 194 league games before deciding to leave the game in 1955, despite still being Cardiff's first choice and playing well. He was later invited to join the Ninian Park club's board of directors, a position he held for nearly 30 years.

EVANS, TONY A former electrician, Tony Evans began his Football League career with Blackpool but never made his mark at Bloomfield Road. He joined Cardiff City in the summer of 1975 and made his début in a 1–0 win at Brighton in the third game of the 1975–76 season. That campaign saw him score 31 goals in 57 matches and top the club's league goalscoring charts with 21 goals as the Bluebirds won promotion to the Second Division. The following season Evans was again the club's leading scorer with 24 goals including all four in a 4–4 draw at Bristol Rovers in a League Cup tie. Evans was hampered by a thigh injury and, though he returned to first-team action in readiness for the 1979–80 campaign, he left Ninian Park after scoring 62 goals in 153 games to join Birmingham City for £120,000. He made a goalscoring début in a 4–3 defeat at Fulham on the opening day of the 1979–80 season, though a series of niggling injuries reduced his appearances during that campaign. He continued to find the net for the Blues and in September 1981 he scored his only hat-trick for the club in a 3–0 home win over Manchester City. Though an occasional lack of control let him down, he scored 33 goals in 76 games for Birmingham. He later played for Crystal Palace, Wolverhampton Wanderers, Bolton Wanderers on loan and Swindon Town before leaving the first-class game.

EVER-PRESENTS A total of 52 Birmingham City players have been ever-present throughout a league season. The greatest

Tony Evans

number of ever-present seasons by a member of the Blues is four, a record held by Arthur 'Nat' Robinson. Next in line come Billy Ollis, Freddie Wheldon and Dan Tremelling with three.

F

FA CUP The club's first game in the FA Cup took place on 17 October 1881 when they beat Derby Town 2–1. In 1885–86 the Blues reached the semi-final of the FA Cup for the first time, beating Burton Wanderers (Home 9–2), Darwen (Home 3–1), Derby County (Home 4–2), Davenham (Away 2–1) and Redcar (Home 2–0) before losing to West Bromwich Albion 4–0 at the Aston Lower Grounds. On 19 November 1898 the Blues recorded their biggest-ever victory in the FA Cup when in a fourth round qualifying match they beat Druids 10–0. The club recorded double figures again the following season, beating Oswestry United 10–2. The club failed to enter the FA Cup in 1921–22 when secretary Sam Richards forgot to send in their application form – consequently they were not in the hat for the first-round draw. The Blues reached the FA Cup final for the first time in 1930–31 with Joe Bradford scoring in every round. After beating Liverpool 2–0 at Anfield, they repeated the scoreline in the fourth round at home to Port Vale. A 3–0 home win over Watford took the Blues into the quarter-final where they met Chelsea. After a 2–2 draw at St Andrew's, the replay at Stamford Bridge attracted a crowd of 74,365 with a further 6,000 locked outside. The Blues won 3–0 with George Briggs having a hand in all three goals. In the semi-final, two goals from Ernie Curtis gave them victory over Sunderland, but at Wembley, despite Joe Bradford again netting for the Blues, the Cup went to West Bromwich Albion who won 2–1. In 1945–46, Birmingham beat the Cup holders Portsmouth 1–0 over two legs and then beat Watford 6–1 on aggregate, Sunderland 3–2 and Bradford 8–2 again over two matches before meeting Derby County in the semi-final. After a 1–1 draw at Hillsborough, the Blues were reduced to 10 men in the replay at Maine Road and lost 4–0. The club reached the semi-finals again in 1950–51 but after beating

Manchester City (Home 2–0), Derby County (Away 3–1), Bristol City (Home 2–0) and Manchester United (Home 1–0), they lost 2–1 to Blackpool at Goodison Park after the first match at Maine Road had been goalless. In 1955–56 the Blues reached their second FA Cup final. Eddie Brown netted a hat-trick in a 7–1 win at Torquay in the third round before victories over Leyton Orient (Away 4–0), West Bromwich Albion (Away 1–0) and Arsenal (Away 3–1) took them to a semi-final meeting with Sunderland at Hillsborough. After a convincing 3–0 win, the Blues met Manchester City in the final at Wembley but, despite Bert Trautmann playing on with a broken neck, the Maine Road club won 3–1. Birmingham reached the semi-finals again the following season but lost 2–0 to Manchester United at Hillsborough. It was 1967–68 before the Blues made it to the last four of the competition again but after beating Halifax Town (Away 4–2), Leyton Orient (Home 3–0), Arsenal (Home 2–1 after a 1–1 draw at Highbury) and Chelsea (Home 1–0) they lost 2–0 to West Bromwich Albion in front of a Villa Park crowd of 60,831. In 1971–72 the Blues not only won promotion from the Second Division but almost reached their third FA Cup final losing 3–0 to mighty Leeds United in the semi-final at Hillsborough. They then won the third-place play-off but two seasons later it was scrapped. The Blues beat Stoke City after a 4–3 penalty shoot-out. The club's last appearance in an FA Cup semi-final came in 1974–75 when the Blues beat Luton Town (Away 1–0), Chelsea (Away 1–0), Walsall (Home 2–1) and Middlesbrough (Home 1–0) before meeting Fulham at Hillsborough. The game was goalless and after a further 90 minutes without a goal in the replay at Maine Road, the tie went into extra-time. There were barely 60 seconds left on the clock when Fulham's John Mitchell scored the winning goal!

FA CUP FINALS

1931 Birmingham City 1 West Bromwich Albion 2

Had Bob Gregg's seventh-minute 'goal' been allowed to stand, the outcome could well have been different. Joe Bradford, who had scored in every round, took to the field with one leg heavily bandaged. Albion took the lead in the 25th minute when 'WG'

Richardson shot past Hibbs after the ball had rebounded into his path following Barkas's tackle. Bradford equalised with a magnificent volley in the 57th minute but straight from the kick-off, 'WG' scored what proved to be Albion's winner following another mistake in the Birmingham defence.

1956 Birmingham City 1 Manchester City 3

Manchester City took the lead as early as the third minute when Don Revie delivered a 40-yard pass to Clarke on the left-wing. Receiving the return pass, he pushed the ball to Joe Hayes whose splendid left-foot volley beat Merrick in the Birmingham goal. A Kinsey equaliser produced a half-time score of 1–1 but the Maine Road club scored a couple of incredible goals in just two minutes. Revie made the first of these for Dyson before Johnstone scored the third and decisive goal. Just 14 minutes from the end, Bert Trautmann made a sensational save at the feet of City's Peter Murphy. Despite being in terrific pain, he persevered until the end of the game and it was only after the final whistle that it was discovered he had broken his neck.

FERRIS, RAY The son of Irish international inside-forward Jack Ferris, Ray had a series of unsuccessful trials with Glentoran, Distillery and Newry Town. In 1938 Brentford signed him as an amateur after discovering him playing for Cambridge Town whilst on holiday. During the Second World War, Ferris 'guested' for both Spurs and West Ham United but towards the end of the hostilities he signed professional forms for Crewe Alexandra. He had made 101 appearances for the Gresty Road club when he was transferred to Birmingham in March 1949 just before the transfer deadline. He made his début in a 1–0 defeat at Liverpool, keeping his place in the side until the end of the season. He continued to be a regular member of the Birmingham side for the next four seasons, making 106 appearances as the club pushed for promotion to the First Division. His performances won him international recognition in the form of three full caps for Northern Ireland. He was in the Irish party that toured Canada in 1953 where sadly he suffered a serious leg injury that forced him to quit the game.

FESTIVAL OF BRITAIN In May 1951, the Blues played four games in the Festival of Britain with the following results – Airdrieonians (Home 3–5), Dinamo Yugoslavia (Home 0–2), Home Farm Dublin (Away 2–1) and Cork Athletic (Away 5–2).

FILLINGHAM, TOM Tom 'Tosha' Fillingham worked at Hucknall Colliery for a number of years playing centre-forward for Bromley FC in the Miners' Welfare League. He later worked in a dye factory and in the summer of 1928 was given a trial by Birmingham. He impressed and was signed on professional forms by the St Andrew's club almost immediately. He worked his way through the ranks before scoring twice on his début in a 4–1 win at Manchester City in April 1930. On his home début a few days later, he scored the only goal of the game against Portsmouth. In 1930–31, Fillingham played in a variety of positions before settling at centre-half. He went on to appear in 189 league and cup games, scoring nine goals before leaving to join Ipswich Town in June 1938. He did not play any competitive football after the Second World War and in 1950, he lost an eye as a result of an injury sustained on the field of play some years earlier.

FIRE On 21 January 1942, the Main Stand at St Andrew's was burned down by a member of the National Fire Service, who threw what he thought was water on to a brazier. The bucket contained petrol and, as the stand went up in flames, all the club's records and playing kit perished along with it!

FIRST DIVISION The Blues have had 11 spells in the First Division. Their first lasted just two seasons before relegation in 1895–96, whilst their second was for one season only in 1901–02. After winning promotion at the first attempt, the club then spent five seasons in the top flight, finishing seventh in both 1904–05 and 1905–06. Following promotion in 1920–21, the Blues then enjoyed their longest spell – 18 seasons – in the First Division before being relegated in 1938–39. After two seasons in the Second Division, the club returned to Division One but were relegated again in 1949–50 after finishing bottom of the league. When they returned to the top flight in 1955–56 they finished sixth, still the club's highest placing in the Football League. However, after that they spent nine seasons battling continually against relegation before the inevitable drop in 1964–65. The club returned to the First Division seven seasons later before relegation in 1978–79. After only one season playing Second Division football, the Blues returned to top-flight action in 1980–81. Again it was a continuous fight to avoid the drop which came four seasons later. The club returned to the First Division for the 1985–86 season but were relegated at the end of it. Following reorganisation, the club spent two seasons in the 'new' First Division before being relegated but, after winning the Second Division Championship, they are now back in Division One, having played the last four seasons there.

FIRST LEAGUE MATCH The Blues found themselves playing their first-ever Football League match on 3 September 1892 when they entertained Port Vale at Muntz Street. The Birmingham side comprised: C.C. Charsley; J.T. Bayley; F. Speller; W. Ollis; C.A.L. Jenkyns; E.J. Devey; J. Hallam; H.R. Edwards; G.F. Short; G.F. Wheldon and T. Hands; The Blues won 5–1: Fred Wheldon scored twice and Short, Hallam and Edwards scored one apiece.

FIRST MATCH The club's first-ever match took place on a cold afternoon in November 1875 against Holte Wanderers from Aston. The Blues were then known as Small Heath Alliance and fielded the following team: W. Edden; A. Wright; F. James; T. James; G. Edden; W. Edmunds (captain); T. Edden; D. Keys; C. Barmore; C. Barr; J. Sparrow and R. Morris. The last-named player was a late introduction when it was discovered that Holte Wanderers had 12 players on the field! David Keys scored the club's first-ever goal in a 1–1 draw.

FLOODLIGHTS The club's floodlights were switched on for the visit of Borussia Dortmund on 31 October 1956, a game watched by a crowd of 45,000, that saw City draw 3–3 with two goals from Bryan Orritt and one from Alex Govan. There were four floodlight pylons, which were rather unusual in that the two on the Tilton Road were 114 feet high like the others but looked much taller because they were sited at the top of the terracing.

FOOTBALL ALLIANCE The Blues were elected to the Football

Alliance in 1889, an organisation which included teams such as Nottingham Forest, Stoke, Sunderland Albion, The Wednesday and local side St George's. The club's first game in the competition saw them beat St George's 3–2 and, though they later beat Nottingham Forest 12–0 with Will Devey scoring six of the goals, they finished tenth out of 12 clubs. They again finished third from bottom in 1890–91, this time with a point less than the previous season. Matters improved in 1891–92, their last season in the competition, and with Fred Wheldon scoring 21 goals in 22 games, the Blues ended the campaign in third place.

FOOTBALL LEAGUE CUP The Football League Cup was introduced in 1960–61 and City were among the leading clubs who chose to enter the competition immediately, though there were a number who decided it wasn't a worthwhile venture. For their first match, the Blues had to travel to Bradford and won 1–0 thanks to a Mike Hellawell goal. They went out in the next round to Plymouth, however, after a replay. In 1962–63 the Blues won the League Cup, beating Doncaster Rovers (Home 5–0), Barrow (Home 5–1 after a 1–1 draw), Notts County (Home 3–2), Manchester City (Home 6–0) and Bury 4–3 on aggregate in the semi-final before playing Aston Villa, also over two legs. In the first leg at St Andrew's, two goals from Ken Leek and another from Jimmy Bloomfield gave the Blues a 3–1 win. The return leg at Villa Park four days later saw the two sides play out a goalless draw, and so the trophy came to St Andrew's. The Blues almost reached a second League Cup final in 1966–67 but, after disposing of Nottingham Forest (Home 2–1 after a 1–1 draw), Ipswich Town (Home 2–1), Grimsby Town (Away 4–2) and Sheffield United (Away 3–2), they were well beaten 7–2 on aggregate in the semi-final by Queen's Park Rangers. The club had another good run in 1973–74 before losing to Plymouth Argyle in the fifth round. Prior to that, both Bob Hatton in a 4–2 win over Blackpool and Bob Latchford in a 3–1 defeat of Ipswich Town, scored hat-tricks. The Blues reached the fifth round again in 1980–81 before losing 3–1 to Liverpool at Anfield. In 1983–84 the club played eight matches in the competition but only reached the fourth round, because the tie against Notts County went to four matches. The club's best performance in recent years came in 1995–96 when they reached the semi-final. Twelve games were played before Leeds United beat the Blues 5–1 on aggregate to end the dream of an all-Brummie final against Aston Villa!

FORMATION The club was founded in 1875 by a group of cricketing enthusiasts who were largely members of Trinity Church, Bordesley. They were determined to continue their sporting relationships throughout the year by forming a football club which they called Small Heath Alliance. The pioneers of the club were Bill Edmunds, who later became the club's first official captain, the James brothers Arthur, Fred and Tom and the Edden brothers Will, George and Tom. Their earliest games were played on wasteland in Arthur Street.

FOSTER, WINSTON Centre-half Winston Foster had a brief spell on the club's ground-staff before turning professional in November 1958. He had to wait until April 1961 before making his first-team début, replacing Trevor Smith in a 1–0 home defeat by Burnley. In 1961 he played against AS Roma in the first leg of the Inter Cities Fairs Cup final and did not let the side down as the Blues fought out a 2–2 draw. Foster replaced Smith on a permanent basis in 1964–65 when he was the club's only ever-present in a season which saw them lose their top-flight status. He had to undergo a cartilage operation and this reduced his number of first-team appearances. He had played in 169 league and cup games when, after a loan spell with Crewe Alexandra, he joined Plymouth Argyle. After appearing in 33 league games for the Home Park club he entered non-league football with Chelmsford City, later playing for Bromsgrove Rovers.

FRAIN, JOHN After forming an effective youth-team full-back pairing with Julian Dicks, he was given his first-team début in a 4–1 defeat at Newcastle United. However, his distribution skills made him a natural for midfield and over the next 10 seasons he appeared in both positions for the club. He missed very few games and after helping the Blues win the Leyland Daf Cup in 1991, he was instrumental in the St Andrew's club winning promotion to the Second Division in 1991–92. Though he was plagued by a series of injuries over the next few seasons, he became the club's longest-serving player and was awarded a well-deserved testimonial for the 1996–97 season. In January 1997, after a loan spell, Frain joined Northampton Town on a permanent basis after having scored 26 goals in 336 games for the Blues. He scored the last-gasp winner for Northampton at Wembley against Swansea that secured the club's promotion to Division Two via the play-offs and, at the time of writing, he has made 77 appearances for the Cobblers.

FRANCIS, KEVIN Nicknamed 'Bigman', 'Inch' and 'Sir', Kevin Francis played for Mile Oak Rangers, a West Midlands Ansells Premier League side before being taken on as a full-time professional by Derby County in 1988. Failing to gain a regular place in the Derby side, he was transferred to Stockport County in February 1991 for £45,000. He claimed five goals in his opening 13 league games for the Edgeley Park club, helping them gain promotion from the Fourth Division. Then, in 1991–92, his presence was vital as County stormed into the promotion play-offs in Division Three only to lose to Peterborough United in the Wembley final. In 1992–93 Francis scored a post-war record 39 goals including his first hat-trick for the club in a 4–3 win at Plymouth Argyle. In 1993–94, Francis netted 34 goals including another hat-trick in a 5–0 home win over Hartlepool United. He left Edgeley Park in January 1995 after scoring 117 goals in 198 games to join Birmingham City for £800,000. Though he was the league's tallest striker at 6ft 7ins, Francis ironically grabbed more goals with his feet than his head. Always a danger at set pieces, he caused so much trouble in and around the opposing penalty area that there always seemed to be a scoring opportunity created when he was in the box. His first game for the Blues came at home to his former club when an own goal helped Birmingham defeat the Cheshire side 1–0. That season the Blues won the Second Division Championship in which Francis scored eight goals in 15 games before suffering serious ligament damage. Although he played only intermittently in 1995–96, he did score some spectacular goals. 1996–97 was no different, and he left St Andrew's after scoring just 21 goals in 94 league and cup games to try his luck with Oxford United.

FRANCIS, TREVOR Plymouth-born Trevor Francis joined the Blues as an apprentice in the summer of 1969 and turned professional in April 1971. He was a member of the City side that

Kevin Francis

reached the quarter-finals of the 1970–71 FA Youth Cup and played for the England Youth team in the Little World Cup in Czechoslovakia that season. He made his first-team début in a 2–0 defeat at Cardiff City in September 1970 at the age of 16 years,

Trevor Francis

139 days old. He scored on his home début the following week as the Blues were held to a 1–1 draw by Oxford United. On 20

February 1971, he became the first 16-year-old to score four goals in a league game when Bolton were beaten 4–0 at St Andrew's. Forming a prolific goalscoring partnership with Bob Latchford, he helped the Blues win promotion to the First Division in 1971–72. He continued to score goals on a regular basis in the top flight with a best of 25 in 1977–78 when he was ever present. After scoring 133 goals in 330 league and cup games, he became Britain's first-ever seven-figure signing when Nottingham Forest paid a reported £1.5 million for his services in February 1979. Despite being plagued by injuries at the City Ground, he scored the winning goal in the 1979 European Cup final against Malmo. Just one week into the 1981–82 season, he joined Manchester City. A year later he was on his way to Sampdoria where he won an Italian Cup winners' medal. After a spell with Atlanta, he signed for Glasgow Rangers. A Skol Cup winners' medal at Ibrox was followed by a return to league football with Queen's Park Rangers. After a year as player-manager at Loftus Road, he took up a similar position with Sheffield Wednesday in June 1991, having joined the club as a player in January 1990. Unlucky to be relegated in 1989–90, Wednesday bounced back immediately the following season after finishing third and won the League Cup. After Ron Atkinson's departure, Francis took over the reins and in his first season, the Owls finished third in the First Division. In 1992–93, Francis took the club to two domestic finals but there was nothing to show for all their efforts except losers' medals. After two seasons of finishing in seventh place in the Premiership, the club ended the 1994–95 season in mid-table and in May 1995 Francis was dismissed. He was appointed Birmingham manager in May 1996, replacing the ebullient Barry Fry. After finishing tenth in 1996–97 and seventh in 1997–98, the club are currently occupying a play-off place in the hope of bringing top-flight football to St Andrew's.

FRY, BARRY An England Schoolboy international, Barry Fry began his career with Manchester United but never made the grade at Old Trafford. After only a handful of league appearances for Bolton Wanderers and Luton Town, he entered non-league football. After a successful career as an attacking midfield player with Bedford Town, where he was renowned for his over-elaborate free-kicks, he entered management with Dunstable and took them to the runners-up spot in the Southern League (North) in 1974–75. After spells in charge of Hillingdon Borough and Bedford Town, he became manager of Barnet. After finishing runners-up in the Conference League three seasons out of four, Fry led them to the title in 1990–91 to enter the Fourth Division. In their first season they led the table but had to settle for the play-offs where they lost to Blackpool. Following a disagreement with chairman Stan Flashman, Fry resigned but was soon reinstated. There was a repeat performance in November 1992 after the club received a heavy fine for keeping their books incorrectly. Fry eventually left Barnet in April 1993 to manage Southend United. His stay at Roots Hall was brief, for in December 1993 he was appointed manager of Birmingham City. Taking with him assistant Edwin Stein and coach David Howell from Southend, he could not prevent the Blues being relegated from the First Division. However, in 1994–95 Fry led the Blues to the Second Division Championship and to success in the Auto Windscreen Shield final at Wembley. In 1995–96 the club reached the semi-final of the League Cup but Fry, who seldom seemed to be off the back pages of the newspapers, paid the price for the club's fall from grace – they finished 15th – with the sack. In May 1996 he was appointed manager of Peterborough United.

FULL MEMBERS CUP After beating Brighton and Hove Albion 3–0 at the Goldstone Ground in the first round of the 1986–87 competition, with goals from Clarke, Kuhl and an own goal by the Seagulls' O'Regan, the Blues travelled to The Valley to play Charlton Athletic. Despite the help of another own goal by Charlton's Peter Shirtliff and a Dave Geddis strike, Birmingham went out of the competition 3–2.

FURLONG, PAUL Paul Furlong began his career with non-league Enfield and in 1988 scored two goals in the FA Trophy final replay against Telford at the Hawthorns. It was this kind of form that led to Coventry City paying £130,000 for his services in the summer of 1991. After just one season at Highfield Road, when he scored five goals in 44 games, he was transferred to Watford for a fee of £250,000. In his first season with the club he topped the scoring charts with 19 goals in 41 games and repeated the feat in 1993–94 with 18 goals in 38 games. He had scored 41 goals in

Paul Furlong

92 games for the Vicarage Road club when Chelsea paid £2.3 million to take him to Stamford Bridge. His opportunities at Chelsea were limited by the signing of Mark Hughes, though when he was given a chance he proved what a wholehearted trier

he was. Big 'Furs' had scored 17 goals in 84 games for Chelsea when he became Birmingham's most expensive signing, moving to St Andrew's for £1.5 million during the 1996 close season. He made his début for City in a 1–0 home win over Crystal Palace on the opening day of the 1996–97 season and went on to appear in more games than any other player at St Andrew's. Though his goal tally of 12 was a little disappointing, his all-round play was appreciated by team-mates and supporters. In 1997–98 he was the club's top scorer with 19 goals including hat-tricks against Stoke City (Away 7–0) and Stockport County (Home 4–1) – the first City player to score two league hat-tricks since Keith Bertschin in 1979–80. The big, powerful striker would surely have scored many more had not injury and suspension forced him to miss 23 of the club's matches!

G

GALLAGHER, JOE A member of the Liverpool Boys team which won the English Schools Trophy in 1970, he immediately signed as an apprentice with Birmingham, turning professional in January 1972. After playing in a Texaco Cup game at Stoke, he made his league début along with former Leeds goalkeeper Gary Sprake at Arsenal in October 1973. He immediately claimed a

Joe Gallagher

regular first-team place, initially playing alongside Kenny Burns at the heart of the Blues' defence. After City's relegation to the Second Division in 1979 they bounced back immediately in 1980, but after another season at St Andrew's, Gallagher, who scored 23 goals in 335 first-team games, was on his way. He joined Wolverhampton Wanderers for £350,000 but after only 34 appearances, he moved to West Ham United in December 1982 for only £25,000. Just six months later he was on the move again, this time to Burnley where, after suffering persistent knee problems, he was advised by a specialist to retire. After taking over as youth-team coach, he suddenly found himself back in the first-team picture following a spate of injuries, and played his part in helping the Clarets cling on to their league status! After a spell in non-league football he returned to St Andrew's in 1990, working on the Community Football programme before becoming manager of Midland Combination club King's Heath.

GEMMILL, ARCHIE Born in Paisley, he began his football career with St Mirren in 1964 before joining Preston North End for £16,000 in June 1967. After three years at Deepdale he moved to Derby County for £60,000 and it was under Brian Clough's management that his career really began to take off. Bringing a competitive edge to every game, he played a significant role in helping the Rams win the League title in 1972 and again in 1975. Gemmill was a non-stop 90-minute competitor, at his best when running with the ball. This industrious side to Gemmill's talent obviously appealed to Clough, for when he was in charge of Forest in 1977–78 he went back to Derby to sign him. At the end of his first campaign at the City Ground he picked up his third Championship medal. In 1978–79 he was instrumental in helping Forest to reach the European Cup final. However, he was on the substitute's bench on the big day and didn't play the game that saw Malmo beaten 1–0 in Munich. A valued member of the Scotland squad, he played 43 times at full level and no one who ever saw his goal against Holland in the 1978 World Cup will ever forget it. In August 1979 he was allowed to leave Forest and join Birmingham City for £150,000. After making his début in the opening game of the 1979–80 season, which the Blues lost 4–3 at home to Fulham, his influence in midfield helped the club win promotion to the First Division. He spent three seasons at St Andrew's, scoring 14

Archie Gemmill

goals in 115 games before joining Wigan Athletic as a non-contract player. A few months later he returned to the Baseball Ground for a second spell. He joined Forest's coaching staff in August 1985 before later sharing the managerial duties at

Rotherham United with former Forest colleague, John McGovern.

GIANT-KILLING Giant-killing epitomises the romance of the FA Cup and in recent years the Blues have been beaten on two occasions at St Andrew's by non-league clubs. On 14 January 1986 the Blues, who were anchored near the foot of the First Division and hadn't won in 17 games, lost 2–1 to Altrincham. The Gola League team's keeper was former City player, Jeff Wealands, but he was rarely troubled. Robert Hopkins had put Birmingham ahead but then, after Ellis had equalised for the visitors, Hopkins found himself under pressure facing his own goal. As David Seaman came out to intercept, Hopkins' intended back pass slid beyond him and into the unguarded net! On 8 January 1994 City played host to Kidderminster Harriers who were top of the GM Vauxhall Conference and managed by lifelong Birmingham fan, Graham Allner. The Blues got off to a perfect start when Paul Harding converted a ninth-minute cross to put them ahead. Cartwright equalised for the visitors just before half-time and then they took the lead in the 63rd minute when Jon Purdie scored from fully 25 yards. City pushed forward in search of an equaliser but it wasn't to be: they hit the post, had shots cleared off the line, had a goal disallowed for offside and missed a penalty!

GLEGHORN, NIGEL Nigel Gleghorn began his league career with Ipswich Town where he made 84 first-team appearances before joining Manchester City in the summer of 1988. After just one season at Maine Road, the Blues splashed out £175,000 to bring him to St Andrew's. He made his début in a 2–0 defeat at Shrewsbury Town in September 1989 and then held his place in the side to appear in all of the remaining 43 games. He missed very few games the following season and appeared for the club in the win over Tranmere Rovers at Wembley in the Leyland Daf Cup final. In 1991–92 he was in outstanding form, top-scoring with 22 league and cup goals as the Blues won promotion from the Third Division. In the early part of the following season, Gleghorn, who had scored 43 goals in 176 games, left to join Stoke City for £100,000. In his first season at the Victoria Ground he helped the Potters win the Third Division Championship and missed very few games over the next four seasons. After switching

Nigel Gleghorn

from the left-wing to the centre of midfield at the start of the 1995–96 season, Gleghorn played in all of the club's 56 games as they lost to Leicester City in the First Division play-offs. He had scored 31 goals in 208 games when he was allowed to join Burnley on a free transfer. Unable to settle at Turf Moor he had loan spells with Brentford and Northampton Town before being released in the summer of 1998.

GLOVER, JOHN John Glover played his early football for West Bromwich Unity, Great Bridge Celtic, Halesowen, Rudge Whitworth FC, Newton Albion and West Bromwich Albion Reserves before joining Blackburn Rovers. He spent two years at Ewood Park before signing for Southern League club New Brompton and in the summer of 1900 he was transferred to Liverpool. A member of the Anfield club's League Championship-winning side of 1900–01, he joined the Blues in January 1904 for a fee of £250. His first game for the club came just 48 hours after he had put pen to paper in a 1–1 draw at Aston Villa. Over the next four seasons Glover was a regular member of the Blues' first team and, despite being on the small side, formed a wonderful full-back partnership with Frank Stokes. He went on to appear in 124 first-team games before leaving the club to join Brierley Hill Alliance.

GOALKEEPERS Birmingham City FC has almost always been extremely well served by its goalkeepers and most of them have been highly popular with the supporters. The club's first outstanding keeper was Chris Charsley who remained an amateur throughout his playing days. An England international, he helped the Blues win the Second Division Championship in 1892–93 before returning to work for the Birmingham police force. Arthur Robinson made 306 appearances for the Blues between 1899 and 1907, twice helping them win promotion from the Second Division. In the first of those promotion-winning seasons, 1900–01, he conceded only 24 goals. Dan Tremelling joined the Blues in 1919 and stayed with the club for 13 years, making 395 league and cup appearances. He won international recognition with England and helped Birmingham win the Second Division Championship in 1920–21. Harry Hibbs was one of the Blues' greatest keepers. Though on the small side, he won 25 caps for England and appeared for Birmingham in the 1931 FA Cup final. Gil Merrick, who later managed the Blues, appeared in 541 games for the club and won 23 caps for England. He helped Birmingham win the League South Championship in 1945–46 and the Second Division title in 1947–48 and 1954–55. Johnny Schofield joined the Blues as cover for Gil Merrick before eventually replacing him at the start of the 1959–60 season. Twice suffering a fractured skull, he was an excellent club man, appearing in 23 games for the

Blues. Jim Herriot, who appeared in FA Cup and League Cup semi-finals during his time at St Andrew's also won eight Scottish international caps before leaving to join Hibernian. Dave Latchford, elder brother of Bob, established himself in the City side during 1972–73 and appeared in a total of 239 games for the club before being replaced by Jim Montgomery. Present England keeper David Seaman joined the Blues from Peterborough United and in a little under two years at St Andrew's appeared in 84 games before signing for Queen's Park Rangers for £200,000. The club's present keeper is Ian Bennett who has appeared in over 200 games for the Blues.

GOALS The most goals Birmingham City have scored in any one league game are their 12–0 victories against Walsall Town Swifts on 17 December 1892 and Doncaster Rovers on 1 April 1903.

GOALS – CAREER BEST The highest goalscorer in the Blues' history is Joe Bradford who netted 267 goals for the club between seasons 1920–21 and 1934–35, 249 in the league and 18 in the FA Cup.

GOALS – INDIVIDUAL Four players have scored five goals in a game for Birmingham. The first was Walter Abbott who netted five of the goals in the club's 8–0 home win over Darwen on 26 November 1898. On 2 March 1901, Bob McRoberts scored five of the goals in the 10–1 defeat of Blackpool. Benny Green scored five as the Blues beat Middlesbrough 7–0 on Boxing Day 1905, whilst the last player to achieve the feat was Jimmy Windridge in the 11–1 rout of Glossop on 23 January 1915.

GOALS – SEASON The club's highest league goalscorer in any one season is still Walter Abbott who scored 34 league goals in 1898–99 including five against Darwen as the Blues finished eighth in the Second Division. He also scored eight goals in the FA Cup including a hat-trick against Port Vale.

GOLDEN GOAL The first Wembley match to be decided by a golden goal was the Auto Windscreen Shield final of 1995, Paul Tait giving Birmingham City the win over Carlisle United, 13 minutes into overtime.

GOODIER, TED A tall, fair-haired wing-half, Ted Goodier was no mean player: he appeared for Oldham Athletic, Queen's Park Rangers, Watford, Crewe and Rochdale, and helped the Scotland club win the Lancashire Senior Cup in 1949. Goodier had a six-month spell in charge at St Andrew's during the 1944–45 season before Birmingham added the 'City' tag. He returned to take charge at Rochdale until 1952 after which he joined Wigan Athletic. The strictest of disciplinarians, Goodier's side gave First Division Newcastle United a real fright in the FA Cup, taking the mighty Magpies to a replay. In 1953–54 the Latics won practically everything there was to win – Lancashire Combination Championship, Lancashire Junior Cup and Makerfield Cup. After a row with Wigan chairman, Sid Littler, he left to take charge of Oldham Athletic. Goodier did not have a happy time at Boundary Park, however, and left after the club entered the newly formed Fourth Division.

GOODWIN, FRED One of the Busby Babes, he was always overshadowed by Duncan Edwards and Eddie Colman at Old Trafford and consequently appearances were rare. After the Munich air disaster, however, he was drafted into the side and soon became a key member. He played in the 1958 FA Cup final but the arrival of Maurice Setters spelt the end of his Old Trafford career and in March 1960 he joined Leeds United for £10,000. Tragically, his career at Elland Road was ended by the triple fracture of a leg in an FA Cup game against Cardiff in January 1964. He later moved to Scunthorpe, missing out on a Leeds revival, and had a spell as manager at Scunthorpe. He later managed Brighton before taking charge at Birmingham City in May 1970. He took the Blues into the First Division in 1971–72 and to two losing FA Cup semi-finals in 1973 and 1975. Goodwin was full of new ideas and introduced yoga, psychological tests and a variety of new training techniques during his time at St Andrew's. He also introduced the club's present manager Trevor Francis to League football. Goodwin switched players around but, despite implementing new tactics and formations, the Blues struggled against relegation from the top flight and only five months after losing to Fulham in the FA Cup semi-final, he was dismissed. He went on to become manager-coach at Minnesota Kicks and during the 1980s he recruited players for the American Indoor League.

GORDON, JOHNNY All-action forward Johnny Gordon signed as an apprentice at Fratton Park from the local Hillside Youth Club in 1947 and, after turning professional, made his league début against Blackpool in August 1951. By 1953–54 he had become a regular in the Pompey side. Often the scorer of two goals in a match – a feat he achieved for Portsmouth on ten occasions – he scored just one hat-trick in a 4–4 draw against Sheffield Wednesday at Hillsborough. Birmingham City were keen to acquire a proven goalscorer and signed him in September 1958 for a fee of £10,000. He marked his début with a goal in a 4–2 home win over Leicester City and in his three seasons with the St Andrew's club, continued to be a regular marksman. His best season was 1959–60 when he netted 19 goals in 43 games, but in March 1961 the love of his home-town team proved too strong and he returned to Fratton Park. In his second spell he helped Pompey win the Third Division Championship in 1962 and went on to score 120 goals in 489 first-team outings.

GOVAN, ALEX Glasgow-born Alex Govan played his early football with Bridgeton Boys' Club before signing professional forms for Plymouth Argyle in the summer of 1946. After only six appearances in the Devon club's Football Combination side, he was selected to make his Football League début against Coventry City. That early promise was not sustained and it was only after playing for the RAF during his National Service that he regained his form and was ready to take his place on the side. By then he had switched from inside-left to the wing and it was as a specialist outside-left that he became a regular first-teamer for three seasons, winning a Third Division (South) Championship medal in 1951–52. He left Home Park to join the Blues in the summer of 1953 and made a goalscoring début on the opening day of the 1953–54 season as Birmingham beat Hull City 2–0. The following season he was the club's second top scorer with 15 goals in 37 league games as the St Andrew's club won promotion to the top flight as champions of the Second Division. In 1956–57, Govan scored five hat-tricks against Portsmouth (Away 4–3), Newcastle United (Home 6–1), Preston North End (Home 3–0), Leeds United (Home 6–2) and Southend United (Away 6–1) in the FA Cup, to establish a club record for a winger in a single campaign. He appeared for the Blues in the 1956 FA Cup final but, after scoring 60 goals in 186 games, he left to join Portsmouth. Within six months he was back at Home Park where he took his tally of goals in his two spells with the club to 38 in 150 games before hanging up his boots.

GREEN, BENNY Benny Green joined the Blues from Barnsley in October 1903 and made his début in a 2–1 home win over Blackburn Rovers. The following season he teamed up with Billy 'Bullet' Jones and the two formed a prolific goalscoring partnership. On Boxing Day 1905, Green scored five of the Blues goals in a 7–0 home win over Middlesbrough and on 29 December 1906 he had the distinction of scoring the club's first-ever goal at St Andrew's in a 3–0 win over Preston North End, for which he won a piano! Following the signings of Freeman, Millington and Needham, the Blues sold Green, who had scored 46 goals in 198 games, to Burnley. He continued to find the net in his two seasons at Turf Moor before moving to Preston in the summer of 1911. He helped the Lilywhites win the Second Division Championship in 1912–13 before ending his career with Blackpool.

GREEN, COLIN Full-back Colin Green began his Football League career with Everton and, on his début, marked Stanley Matthews, in a 4–1 win at Blackpool. He had made only 15 league appearances for the Goodison Park club when Birmingham paid £12,000 for his services in December 1962. Green made his City début in a 2–0 home defeat by Tottenham Hotspur later that month and at the end of his first season at St Andrew's, he won a League Cup winners' tankard after the Blues had beaten Aston Villa in the two-legged final. Green's performances over the next few seasons led to his winning 15 full caps for Wales, the first against USSR in 1965. His full-back partners were numerous – Stan Lynn, Ray Martin and Bobby Thomson – but no matter who it was, he always formed a fine understanding. Green, who suffered a broken leg in 1966, was a regular in the City side until the end of the 1968–69 season when another injury cost him his first-team place. His only goal in his 217 appearances for the club was the winner in a 3–2 victory at Carlisle United in September 1968. After leaving St Andrew's, he had a short loan spell with Wrexham before ending his playing career with non-league Tamworth.

GREEN, KEN Ken Green was playing as an amateur with Millwall when he wrote to the St Andrew's club to ask for a trial. After a series of impressive performances, City signed him in 1943 and he made seven wartime appearances before being posted abroad. After the hostilities were over, he returned to St Andrew's and made his league début in a 2–1 win at Brentford in September 1947. Able to play on either flank, the full-back was a regular first-team member for the next 11 seasons, being ever present in 1952–53. He went on to appear in 442 league and cup games, helping the club win the Second Division title on two occasions – 1947–48 and 1954–55 – and reach the FA Cup final in 1956 where they lost 3–1 to Manchester City. Green won England 'B' honours and represented the Football League.

GREGG, BOB Inside-forward Bob Gregg was born in Ferryhill, County Durham, and played for a number of local sides before signing professional forms for Darlington in the summer of 1924. He had to wait two seasons before making his début for the Quakers but was so impressive that Sheffield Wednesday signed him in May 1928. He made a good start with the Hillsborough club but was hampered by a series of injuries and, in two and a half years with the Owls, he scored seven goals in 39 appearances. He joined Birmingham for a fee of £2,200 in January 1931 and made his début in a 2–1 home defeat by Derby County. He ended the season with three goals in 15 games including one against his former club as the Blues beat Wednesday 2–0. That season he was a member of the Birmingham side that played West Bromwich Albion in the FA Cup final and had a 'goal' disallowed for offside in the 2–1 defeat. His best season for the club was 1932–33 when he scored nine goals in 39 games including a hat-trick in a 3–0 win over Liverpool. He had scored 13 goals in 75 league and cup games when he left to join Chelsea in September 1933. After appearing in 51 games for the Stamford Bridge club, he played non-league football for Boston United before ending his career during the Second World War with League of Ireland club, Sligo Rovers.

GROSVENOR, TOM Born at Netherton near Dudley in November 1908, Tom Grosvenor began playing football with a team known as Tippity Green Vics before turning out for Vono

Works where he was employed. He went to Stourbridge before joining Birmingham in March 1928. He had to wait until October 1931 before he made his first-team début in a 2–0 defeat at Middlesbrough. After that he was a regular member of the side and in 1932–33 he was ever present. His form the following season led to his winning representative honours with the Football League and three full international caps for England in which he scored a couple of goals. In February 1936, after scoring 18 goals in 116 first-team outings and creating many more for Joe Bradford, Grosvenor was transferred to Sheffield Wednesday for £2,500. He was unable to command a place in what was a struggling team and in June 1937 he joined Bolton Wanderers. He missed only one game in his first season with the Lancashire club but retired during the war after 'guesting' for Walsall. His brother Percy was also a professional footballer with Leicester City.

GUEST, BILLY In August 1928, the Brierley Hill-born winger joined the St Andrew's ground-staff at the age of 14 before turning professional three years later. He played his first game for the club in a 1–1 draw at Arsenal on the opening day of the 1933–34 season before establishing himself as a first-team regular midway through the following campaign. However, it was during his first season in the side that Guest, who was not a prolific scorer, had his best game for the club. The Blues were languishing near the foot of the First Division and were in desperate need of points when they travelled to a very muddy Filbert Street to take on Leicester City. Guest scored a magnificent hat-trick and the Blues won a remarkable game 7–3. He had scored 17 goals in 84 league and cup games when he was allowed to leave St Andrew's and join West Ham United. His stay at Upton Park was short and in January 1937 he moved to Blackburn Rovers. He played at Wembley in the 1940 Wartime League Cup final when the Lancashire club were beaten 1–0 by West Ham. He 'guested' for Birmingham along with a number of other clubs during the Second World War before ending his league career with Walsall.

GUEST PLAYERS The 'guest' system was used by all clubs during the two wars. Although at times it was abused almost beyond belief (in that some sides that opposed the Blues had 10 or 11 'guests'!) it normally worked sensibly and effectively to the benefit of players, clubs and supporters alike. The most distinguished players to 'guest' for the Blues in the First World War were Charlie Buchan (Sunderland), Jesse Pennington (West Bromwich Albion), Harry Hampton (Aston Villa) and Sammy Brooks (Wolves). In the Second World War, players of the calibre of Eddie Hapgood (Arsenal), George Hardwick (Middlesbrough) and Peter Doherty (Manchester City) turned out for the Blues.

H

HALL, JACK After trials with Nottingham Forest and Mansfield Town, the Hucknall-born forward signed professional forms for Stoke in 1904 but within a couple of seasons he had left the Victoria Ground to continue his career with Brighton. In April 1908, he left the south-coast club and joined Middlesbrough but again, after two years, he was on the move, this time to Leicester Fosse. He failed to settle with his new club and in December 1910 he joined Birmingham. In his first game for the St Andrew's club he scored the winning goal in a 2–1 home defeat of Huddersfield Town and then proceeded to score in each of the next six games. He ended the season as the club's top scorer with 13 goals in 19 games. In 1911–12 he once again headed the club's scoring charts with 21 goals in 35 games including hat-tricks against Wolverhampton Wanderers (Home 3–1) and Clapton Orient (Home 4–0). He also netted all four goals in a 4–3 home win over Leeds City. Over the next three seasons, however, the powerfully built forward suffered a series of injury problems and at the end of the 1914–15 season – after which he had scored 48 goals in 103 first-team games – he was forced to retire.

HALL, JEFF Though he didn't consider himself good enough for league football, Jeff Hall signed professional forms for Birmingham City in May 1950. After being converted from right-half to full-back and turning in a number of solid performances for the club's reserve side, he made his first-team début in a 3–3 draw at home to Bury in January 1951. After a handful of appearances the following season, he established himself as a first-team regular in 1952–53 and the following season scored his only goal for the club in a 3–2 defeat at Stoke when he was asked to play at outside-right in an emergency. He helped the Blues win the Second Division Championship in 1954–55 and reach the FA

Cup final the following season. That season also saw him win the first of 17 full caps for England when he played in a 5–1 win over Denmark in Copenhagen. Hall had appeared in 265 league and cup games for Birmingham when he contracted polio and died at the tragically young age of 29 on 4 April 1959. A Jeff Hall memorial scoreboard and clock were erected at the City End of St Andrew's to commemorate a player whose death was a sad loss to both Birmingham City and England.

HAMPTON, HARRY Known as the 'Wellington Whirlwind', Harry Hampton scored 54 goals in his two seasons for his home-town club before joining Aston Villa in May 1904. He stayed with the club until February 1920, scoring 242 goals in 373 league and cup matches. His total of 215 league goals remains the club record. He scored 14 hat-tricks, including five goals when Villa beat Sheffield Wednesday 10–0 on 5 October 1912 and both goals when they won the FA Cup in 1905 beating Newcastle United 2–0. He won another FA Cup winners' medal in 1913 and a League Championship medal in 1909–10 when he topped the club's goalscoring charts with 26 goals in 32 league matches. He was capped four times by England, winning his first against Scotland in 1913. Hampton owed many of his goals to the fine crosses of Brawn, Hall and Wallace, and made his name by charging the opposition goalkeeper, many of whom ended up in the back of the net with the ball! After leaving Villa Park to join the Blues, he made his début at Barnsley, scoring twice in a 5–0 win. He ended that campaign with 11 goals in ten league games including four in an 8–0 home win over Nottingham Forest. The following season he was the club's leading scorer as they won the Second Division Championship. Included in his total of 16 goals in 29 games was a hat-trick in a 5–0 defeat of Leicester City. He had scored 31 goals in 59 games for the Blues when he left St Andrew's in September 1922 to join Newport County. Two years later he returned to Wellington before ending his involvement in the game with a spell as coach at Preston North End.

HARFORD, MICK Much-travelled striker Mick Harford began his career with Lincoln City and after topping the club's scoring charts in his first two seasons with the Imps, he left to join Newcastle United for £180,000, still the record fee received by

Mick Harford

the Sincil Bank club. He failed to settle at St James Park and therefore joined Bristol City but the Robins were on the verge of bankruptcy and could not meet the instalments on his transfer fee. Newcastle appealed to the Football League, who ordered Bristol City to return Harford to Newcastle on a free transfer.

The Ashton Gate club immediately sold him to Birmingham City, the transfer fee of £100,000 being paid to Newcastle United rather than his current club. After scoring the only goal of the game on his début against Brighton, he went on to find the net nine times in 12 games at the end of the 1981–82 season, earning priceless points which saved the Blues from relegation to the Second Division. In 1982–83, City again staved off relegation by winning five and drawing one of their last six games with Harford scoring match-winning goals in three of them. After scoring 33 goals in 109 games he was transferred to Luton Town where he was to enjoy the best years of his career. In 1988 he won a League Cup winners' medal but after scoring 81 goals in 186 games he made the surprise move from Kenilworth Road to Derby County. After being unable to halt the Rams' slide to relegation in 1991, he returned to Luton where he took his tally of goals to 93 before signing for Chelsea. He later played for his home-town club Sunderland and Coventry City before joining Wimbledon where he is now coach.

HARRIS, FRED Fred Harris scored on his début in a 2–1 home win over Aston Villa on the opening day of the 1934–35 season. The following campaign saw him top the club's scoring charts with 17 goals and again in 1938–39 when the club were relegated to the Second Division. His total of 14 goals included his first hat-trick for the club in a 4–3 defeat at home to Charlton Athletic. During the early part of the war he joined the Auxiliary Police Reserve and, in 1941, he was injured in an air-raid on Birmingham. He later 'guested' for Chester and was a reserve for England as well as appearing in 104 wartime games for the Blues. When league football resumed in 1946–47, Harris was made captain and switched from his inside-forward position to right-half. In 1947–48 he missed just two games as the Blues won the Second Division Championship. He went on to score 69 goals in 310 league and cup games before hanging up his boots and qualifying as a masseur and physiotherapist, and a chiropodist.

HARRIS, JIMMY Birkenhead-born Jimmy Harris was a member of the district's successful schoolboy side before joining Everton as an amateur. He later turned professional and made his first-team début in a 1–0 win at Burnley in August 1955, replacing Dave

Hickson. Harris kept his place in the side, appearing in all 40 remaining games and top-scoring with 19 league goals, along with another four in the FA Cup. Midway through his first season with the club he won England Under-23 honours when he played against Scotland at Hillsborough. In 1958–59 Harris scored a hat-trick in the match against Tottenham Hotspur at White Hart Lane but still ended up on the losing side as Everton went down 10–4. In December 1960, after scoring 72 goals in 207 league and cup games, Harris left Goodison Park to join Birmingham City for £20,000. His first game for the St Andrew's club was in the Fairs Cup when he scored in a 5–0 win over Boldklub, Copenhagen. His first league game was against his former club, Everton, at St Andrew's, an entertaining game which the Toffees won 4–3. Harris ended his first season at the club as top scorer with 13 league and cup goals. He repeated the feat in 1961–62 with 20 goals and went on in four seasons with the club to net 53 goals in 115 first-team outings. His only honour whilst with the Blues was a League Cup winners' tankard in 1962–63 as Aston Villa were beaten in the two–legged final. In July 1964 he joined Oldham Athletic, moving to Tranmere Rovers two years later. Unable to break into the Prenton Park club's first team, he hung up his boots.

HATTON, BOB A consistent goalscorer wherever he played, Bob Hatton had already enjoyed a varied career with Wolves, Bolton Wanderers, Northampton Town and Carlisle United before he arrived at St Andrew's in October 1971 for a club record fee of £82,500. Hatton made his début in a 1–1 draw at Burnley and spent five years with the Blues, his longest spell with one club. In his first season he scored 15 goals in 26 league games to help the Blues into the First Division and netted some important goals in the run-up to the FA Cup semi-final. He was the club's leading scorer in 1973–74 and netted his only hat-trick for the club in a 4–2 League Cup defeat of Blackpool. He topped the goalscoring charts again in 1974–75, thriving on the pin-point crosses of Gordon Taylor. He had scored 73 goals in 218 first-team games when he left St Andrew's in the summer of 1976 to sign for Blackpool. Though he only spent two seasons at Bloomfield Road, he scored 35 goals in 84 games and, in 1977–78, he scored four goals in a 5–2 win over Blackburn Rovers and hat-tricks against Orient (Away 4–1), Cardiff City (Home 3–0) and Charlton Athletic (Home 5–1). At the end of that season, he moved to Luton Town and ended his league career with Sheffield United and Cardiff City, totalling 217 goals in 620 league games altogether. He later had a spell in the League of Ireland with Dundalk.

HAT-TRICKS Though Will Devey scored a double hat-trick in the club's 12–0 win over Nottingham Forest in their first season in the Football Alliance, it was Billy Walton who had the distinction of scoring the Blues' first hat-trick in the Football League in a 12–0 win over Walsall Town Swifts. The only Birmingham player to score a hat-trick on his league début is Peter Murphy who netted three goals in a 5–0 win at Doncaster Rovers on 19 January 1952. Alex Govan equalled Joe Bradford's feat of scoring four hat-tricks in a season in 1956–57 and Geoff Vowden is the club's only substitute to score a hat-trick after coming off the bench. He did this in a 5–1 win over Huddersfield Town in September 1968. Joe Bradford holds the club record for the most hat-tricks with a total of 13. The last Birmingham player to score a hat-trick is Paul Furlong in the 7–0 win at Stoke City on 10 January 1998.

HELLAWELL, MIKE Keighley-born winger Mike Hellawell had a trial with Huddersfield Town before joining Queen's Park Rangers in the summer of 1955. He scored eight goals in 48 games for the Loftus Road club and in 1957 played for the Third Division (South) against the Third Division (North). He joined the Blues in May 1957 and scored on his début four months later in a 4–1 home defeat by Newcastle United. It was his only appearance that season and, after making just one more appearance in 1958–59, he began to establish himself in the City side the following season after Harry Hooper's departure to Sunderland. He played in the 1961 Fairs Cup final after he had scored 10 goals in 28 games during the 1960–61 season to become the club's joint-top scorer. The following season he was ever present, his performances winning him two full caps for England against France and Northern Ireland, both in October 1962. In January 1965, Hellawell, who had scored 33 goals in 213 games, joined Sunderland. In the summer of 1966 he moved to Huddersfield Town, later ending his league career with Peterborough United. He finally entered non-league football with Bromsgrove Rovers before hanging up his boots.

HENNESSEY, TERRY A cultured wing-half, Terry Hennessey was given his Birmingham City début by the club's new manager Gil Merrick in March 1961 in a 3–2 home win over Manchester City. In 1962–63 he won a League Cup winners' tankard and was voted the Midland Footballer of the Year. In that season he was the club's only ever-present and over the six seasons he played at St Andrew's he missed very few matches. He had played in 202 first-team games for the Blues when he left to join Nottingham Forest. Though he was only 23 when he arrived at the City Ground, he looked much older because of his receding hairline. Showing a great maturity in his play, the Welsh-born player won 39 caps for his country. In 1966–67 he was appointed Forest's captain and led the Reds to an FA Cup semi-final where they lost 2–1 to Spurs and to runners-up spot in the First Division. In February 1970 he joined Derby County as the Rams' first £100,000 signing, and in 1971–72 he won a League Championship medal. After injury cut short his playing career the following season, he managed non-league Tamworth and Kimberley Town before coaching Tulsa Roughnecks in the NASL.

HERRIOT, JIM Goalkeeper Jim Herriot began his career with Dunfermline Athletic. He spent seven seasons at East End Park where he had replaced Eddie Connachan who was sold to Middlesbrough. During his time there, Herriot produced performances that won him international recognition for Scotland at 'B' and Under-23 level. He joined Birmingham in May 1965 for a fee of £17,000 and made his début in a 2–1 home win over Crystal Palace on the opening day of the 1965–66 season. He was ever present the following season and was the club's first-choice keeper for five seasons. Whilst with the Blues he won eight full caps for Scotland and when he replaced Liverpool's Tommy Lawrence against Wales, at Wrexham in May 1969, he became one of only two goalkeeping substitutes to appear in an international match. He played for Birmingham in the 1967 League Cup and 1968 FA Cup semi-finals but in the summer of 1971, after playing in 212 league and cup games for the St Andrew's club, he returned to Scotland to play for Hibernian. With Hibs he appeared in the

Scottish Cup final in 1972, having already played in the 1965 final with Dunfermline and in 1973 won a League Cup winners' medal with the Easter Road club.

HIBBITT, TERRY Few players have made such a dramatic entry into League football as Terry Hibbitt. Coming on as a substitute, the Bradford-born youngster scored for Leeds United with his first touch of the ball. In his early days at Elland Road he was a member of the shadow squad, used as cover to the international players in Don Revie's reign as manager. In August 1971 he joined Newcastle United for £30,000 and starred with the Magpies for four seasons. He played in their side which reached the 1974 FA Cup final but was then sidelined through injury which threatened to end his career. In September 1975, a £100,000 move took him to Birmingham City and he made his début in a 1–1 home draw against Queen's Park Rangers. He was a first-team regular for the St Andrew's club for three seasons, being ever present in 1976–77, but after scoring 11 goals in 122 games he returned to Newcastle in May 1978 in an exchange deal involving Stewart Barraclough. A persistent knee injury forced him to give up League football and he left to run a newsagent's business. In the meantime, he played for Gateshead and had a spell as their player–coach. His younger brother Kenny, an England Under-23 international, gave sterling service to Wolves, Coventry and Bristol Rovers. Terry Hibbitt died from cancer at the age of 47 in August 1994.

HIBBS, HARRY Harry Hibbs, England's number one goalkeeper between the wars, began his career as a centre-forward, leading the attack for Wilnecote Youth before switching to a goalkeeping role at the age of 17 with Tamworth Castle in the Birmingham and District League. The Blues were sufficiently impressed with his progress and in May 1924 they offered him a full-time professional contract. He made his début on the last day of the 1925–26 season in the game against Arsenal at Highbury, a match the Blues lost 3–0. He fared even worse on his one appearance the following season when Tottenham Hotspur beat the Blues 6–1. It was whilst Hibbs was serving his apprenticeship in the club's reserve side that he developed the powers of anticipation that enabled him to get his body behind even the hardest shots from the most acute angles. The 1929–30 season saw Hibbs replace Dan Tremelling in the

Terry Hibbitt

club's first team. He made 33 appearances that term and earned an international trial. In November of the following season he was selected for England against Wales at Stamford Bridge, a game the home side won 6–0. Between this first cap in 1929 and his last against Wales at Molineux in 1936, Harry Hibbs played in 25 of England's 33 internationals and was only on the losing side five times. He was on the losing side in the 1931 FA Cup final against West Bromwich Albion when his opposite number, his cousin Harold Pearson, scored a goal against him. In his 15 seasons with the Blues, Harry Hibbs missed only a few matches through injury, until the 1938–39 season when he was out of the side from October to April and managed only 13 appearances. His last appearance for the St Andrew's club was his wartime benefit match against Aston Villa on 13 April 1940 when City won 2–1. Besides his international honours, he appeared for the Football League three times and took part in an unofficial international against South Africa in 1929. In all, he made 388 league and cup appearances for Birmingham before being appointed manager of Walsall in the summer of 1944. He left in June 1951 and then from February 1953 had a couple of seasons with de Havilands FC in Birmingham. He returned to the game as manager of Ware Town in August 1960 and later took charge of Welwyn Garden City FC.

HOCKEY, TREVOR Much-travelled midfielder Trevor Hockey began his career with Bradford City but in November 1961, after making 53 league appearances for the Valley Parade club, he joined Nottingham Forest. After two years at the City Ground, he switched to Newcastle United and it was from here in November 1965 that the Blues secured his services for a fee of £25,000. He made his début for Birmingham in a 1–0 home defeat at the hands of Coventry City. He missed very few games for the Blues over the next six seasons, going on to score 13 goals in 231 games before leaving to join Sheffield United in January 1971. With the Blades, he won the first of nine full caps for Wales. He later had a spell with Norwich City before returning to Bradford City where he ended his league career. Hockey had scored 28 goals in 523 league games for his various clubs before becoming player-manager of Athlone Town. Hockey later managed Stalybridge Celtic but in 1987, at the age of 43, he died whilst taking part in a five-a-side competition in his home town of Keighley.

HOME MATCHES The Blues have won two Football League matches by a 12–0 scoreline – Walsall Town Swifts on 17 December 1892 and Doncaster Rovers on 11 April 1903. The club have also scored double figures on a further five occasions, beating Glossop 11–1 in 1914–15, Druids 10–0 in the FA Cup of 1898–99, Blackpool 10–1 in 1900–01, Ardwick 10–2 in 1893–94 and Oswestry United 10–2 in the FA Cup of 1899–1900. The club's worst home defeat is 7–1, a scoreline inflicted on the Blues by Burnley in 1925–26 and West Bromwich Albion in 1959–60. The only other club to score seven goals against City at St Andrew's is Sunderland who beat the Blues 7–2 on 13 April 1936.

HOME SEASONS Birmingham City have gone through a complete league season with an undefeated home record on three occasions – 1892–93, 1902–03 and 1971–72. In the 1902–03 season, the club won all 17 of its home games. This is also the club's highest number of home wins, a feat they also achieved in 1946–47.

HONOURS The major honours achieved by the club are:

Division 2 Champions	1892–93	1920–21	1947–48
	1954–55	1994–95	
Division 2 Runners-up	1893–94	1900–01	1902–03
	1971–72	1984–85	
Division 3 Runners-up	1991–92		
FA Cup Runners-up	1931	1956	
League Cup Winners	1963		
Leyand Daf Winners	1991		
Auto Windscreen Winners	1995		
Fairs Cup Runners-up	1959–60	1960–61	

HOOPER, HARRY The son of West Ham's trainer, Harry Hooper senior, Hooper junior made his league début for the Hammers in a 4–2 home win over Barnsley in February 1951. While at Upton Park, the speedy winger played six times for England 'B', twice for England Under-23s and also for the Football League but though he was selected for the full England squad he never played in a full international. During six seasons at Upton Park, he scored 44 goals in 130 games with 1955–56 his best season in terms of goals scored – he netted 16 goals in 36 games including a hat-trick in a 6–1 home win over Doncaster Rovers. In March 1956, Wolverhampton Wanderers paid £25,000 for his services and he scored 19 goals in 39 games for the Molineux club. Midway through Wolves' 1957–58 Championship-winning season, he joined Birmingham City for a fee of £19,500 and made his league début against Manchester United at St Andrew's in a match that ended all-square at 3–3. He appeared for the Blues in the 1960 Inter Cities Fairs Cup final and scored in the first three games of the 1960–61 season to take his tally of goals for Birmingham to 42 – but after making 119 appearances, he moved to Sunderland. He ended his league career with the Wearsiders before playing non-league football for Kettering Town.

HOPKINS, ROBERT Robert Hopkins made his league début for Aston Villa but after just three appearances, two as a substitute, he moved to St Andrew's in March 1983. He made his City début in a 3–0 home win over Notts County and held his place in the side for the remaining 11 games of the season. The winger was a regular member of the Birmingham side over the next two seasons which saw the club both relegated in 1983–84 and winning promotion in 1984–85 when Hopkins scored nine goals and created many more for Clarke and Geddis. Following the club's relegation in 1985–86, he left to join Manchester City but was unable to settle there, and within two months he was back in the Midlands with West Bromwich Albion. He scored 11 goals in 83 league games for the Baggies before returning to St Andrew's for a second spell in March 1989. He took his tally of goals for the club to 34 in 203 first-team games before leaving to play for Shrewsbury Town. He later played in Hong Kong for Instant Dict, before returning home to turn out for Solihull Borough.

HUGHES, BILLY Llanelli-born full-back Billy Hughes began his career with his home-town club before signing for the Blues in the summer of 1935. He was just 17 years old when he made his first-team début in an FA Cup third-round replay at home to Barnsley, which the Yorkshire club won 2–0. It was 1937–38 before he fully established himself in the Birmingham side, his performances earning him the first of 10 full caps for Wales when he played against England in 1938. During the war years he appeared in 55 games for Birmingham and 'guested' for a number of clubs including Arsenal, Spurs and West Ham United. He appeared in 14 unofficial internationals and in 1946 played for Great Britain against the Rest of Europe at Hampden Park. He was still a regular in the Birmingham side when league football resumed in 1946–47. He had appeared in 110 league and cup games for the Blues when in March 1948 he joined Chelsea for a fee of £12,000. On leaving Stamford Bridge, he played for Hereford United and later Flint Town where he won a Welsh Cup medal in 1954.

HUNDRED GOALS Birmingham City have scored more than 100 league goals in a season on just one occasion. That was in 1893–94 when the club scored 103 goals from just 28 matches in a season which saw them runners-up to Liverpool in Division Two. The leading goalscorers were Frank Mobley with 24 goals and Fred Wheldon with 22 goals. The club's best victories were against Ardwick (Home 10–2), Northwich Victoria (Home 8–0 and Away 7–0), Lincoln City (Home 6–0), Port Vale (Home 6–0), Burton Swifts (Home 6–1) and Crewe Alexandra (Home 6–1).

HYND, ROGER Falkirk-born centre-half Roger Hynd was on Glasgow Rangers' books before moving south of the border to play for Crystal Palace. After just one season at Selhurst Park, he left to join the Blues in the summer of 1970 and made his début in a 2–1 home win over Queen's Park Rangers on the opening day of the 1970–71 season. He missed just two games of a campaign in which City finished seventh in Division Two. The following season he was ever present as the Blues finished runners-up to Norwich City to win promotion to the First Division. In 1972–73, Hynd was again one of the club's most consistent performers as the Blues ended their first season back in Division One in mid-table. Hynd had scored nine goals in 198 games when, following a loan spell with Oxford United, he joined Walsall in December 1975. He gave the Saddlers three years' good service before hanging up his boots.

I

INJURIES The risk of serious injury is an ever-present threat in the game of football and all professional players expect to miss games through injury at some point in their careers. One of the most unusual injuries sustained by a Birmingham player befell Colin Gordon who, in September 1989, was forced to miss several matches due to blood poisoning – contracted when a Swansea City player accidently bit into his arm! Birmingham goalkeeper Johnny Schofield survived both a pit explosion at Baddesley Colliery in 1957 and a fractured skull whilst playing for the Blues against Manchester United to appear in 237 games.

INTER CITIES FAIRS CUP The club's European history is strongly linked with the Inter Cities Fairs Cup since they appeared in the first four competitions. Acting as trailblazers for all the English success in Europe that followed, the Blues played their first match in the competition just 10 days after losing 3–1 to Manchester City in the 1956 FA Cup final. The first Inter Cities Fairs Cup was something of a cumbersome affair that took three years to complete! There were 11 teams in the competition (though this was reduced to 10 when Vienna withdrew); England were represented by a City and a London Select invitation team; the entrants were divided into four groups with the winners of each group progressing to the semi-finals. City were placed in quite a difficult group with Dynamo Zagreb and Inter Milan. Their first game was a 0–0 draw away at Inter Milan, from where they travelled to play Zagreb and recorded a 1–0 victory thanks to an Eddie Brown goal. It was seven months later that the Blues played the return against Zagreb – winning 3–0 – and a further four months before they played their return match against Inter Milan. The Blues won this game 2–1 with Alex Govan scoring both City goals. This qualified them for a semi-final meeting with

Barcelona. In the first leg at St Andrew's, Birmingham beat the famous Spanish side 4–3 thanks to a brace of goals by Peter Murphy and one each by Brown and Orritt. In Spain, Barcelona won the return 1–0 which meant a third match at Basle. Sadly, Murphy's solitary strike was not enough and the Blues went down 2–1 to the eventual tournament winners. However, the club were undaunted and entered the next Fairs Cup which ran over two seasons from 1958 to 1960 and was based on a knockout system over two legs. This time the Blues reached the final without losing a match. They eliminated Cologne (Home 2–0 Away 2–2), Dinamo Zagreb (Home 1–0 Away 3–3) and Union St Gilloise (Home 4–2 Away 4–2). City were, in fact, the first British club side to reach the final of a European competition, for the London side who had played Barcelona in the previous final had been a representative side made up of players of half a dozen teams. In the final, City met the holders, Barcelona. On a rain-swept night at St Andrew's, a crowd of 40,524 saw the Blues play out a goalless draw against the Spanish giants, but in the return City found themselves two goals down after six minutes and eventually lost 4–1 with Harry Hooper scoring a late consolation goal. In 1960–61, the Blues continued their exploits in the competition and, after beating Ujpest Dozsa (Home 3–2 Away 2–1) and Boldklub Copenhagen (Home 5–0 Away 4–4), they met their first-ever European opponents Inter Milan in the semi-final. In what must surely rank as one of the best performances by any English club in Europe, City won both legs 2–1 with Jimmy Harris scoring three of the club's goals. Their opponents in the final were AS Roma, the tie being held over until early in the 1961–62 season. A crowd of only 21,005 saw City draw 2–2 in the first leg with goals from Hellawell and Orritt, but their hopes of lifting the trophy were dashed when they lost 2–0 in a bad-tempered second leg in the Italian capital. City got a bye in the first round of the following season's competition but progressed no further than the second round. They slumped to their worst-ever European defeat in the first leg, losing 5–2 at the hands of Spanish club, Español. In the return, a Bertie Auld goal gave the Blues a 1–0 win but it wasn't enough to take them further in the competition. In four seasons in the Inter Cities Fairs Cup, the Blues reached two finals and one semi-final, winning 14 and drawing 6 of 25 games played. In fact, the only home ties they failed to win were the first legs of both finals.

INTERNATIONAL PLAYERS Birmingham City's most capped player (that is, caps gained while players were registered with the club) is Malcolm Page who won 28 caps for Wales. The following is a complete list of players who have gained full international honours for England, Scotland, Wales, Northern Ireland and the Republic of Ireland.

England		Scotland	
Gordon Astall	2	Kenny Burns	8
Percy Barton	7	Johnny Crosbie	1
Joe Bradford	12	Cornelius Dougall	1
Chris Charsley	1	Archie Gemmill	10
Walter Corbett	3	Jim Herriot	8
Trevor Francis	12	Francis McGurk	1
Tom Grosvenor	3	**Wales**	
Jeff Hall	17	Jason Bowen	1
Mike Hellawell	2	Ernie Curtis	2
Harry Hibbs	25	Don Dearson	3
Gil Merrick	23	George Edwards	6
Trevor Smith	2	Leonard Evans	1
Lewis Stoker	3	Colin Green	15
Dan Tremelling	1	Terry Hennessey	16
Republic of Ireland		Billy Hughes	10
Gary Breen	9	Caesar Jenkyns	4
Eric Barber	1	Charlie Jones	2
Tommy Carroll	9	Fred Jones	1
Gerry Daly	5	Noel Kinsey	3
Don Givens	14	Ken Leek	5
James Higgins	1	Andrew Legg	4
Dave Langan	10	Seymour Morris	5
Northern Ireland		Malcolm Page	28
Bobby Brennan	3	Aubrey Powell	1
John Brown	3	Tony Rees	1
Ray Ferris	3	David Richards	6
Jon McCarthy	3	John Roberts	15
		Gary Sprake	5
		Byron Stevenson	4

The first Birmingham player to be capped was Caesar Jenkyns who played for Wales against England on 5 March 1892.

ISLIP, ERNIE Sheffield-born inside-forward Ernie Islip played his early football with his home-town club, Sheffield Douglas, before joining Huddersfield Town in the summer of 1919. In four seasons with the Terriers he scored 26 goals in 98 games and helped the club win promotion to Division One in his first season at Leeds Road. He had played in just three games of the Yorkshire club's League Championship-winning season of 1923–24 when the Blues paid £1,500 to secure his services in November 1923. He scored on his début in a 2–0 home win over West Ham United and though he had played the best football of his career at Huddersfield, he was still a big favourite with the Birmingham fans. His best season in terms of goals scored was 1924–25 when he was the club's joint-top scorer with Joe Bradford. He went on to score 24 goals in 89 games before losing his place to George Briggs. In the summer of 1927 he joined Bradford City but after just one season at Valley Parade, he left to play non-league football for Ashton National.

J

JACKSON, ALEC Able to play in any forward position, Alec Jackson began his career with West Bromwich Albion, signing amateur forms in May 1954 and turning professional some four months later. He made his début for the Baggies in October 1954, scoring in a game at Charlton Athletic, and over the next ten seasons he appeared in 192 league games, scoring 50 goals. Though he broke his leg in Albion's goalless draw against Spurs at White Hart Lane in April 1958, he recovered to win selection for the Football League. He joined Birmingham in the summer of 1964 and made his début in a 4–3 defeat at Nottingham Forest on the opening day of the 1964–65 season. Sadly the Blues lost their First Division status at the end of that campaign but in 1965–66, Jackson was one of the club's better players as they finished tenth in the Second Division. Once again injury kept him out of the opening games of the following season and he left St Andrew's to join Walsall having made 85 appearances for the Blues. His stay at Fellows Park was brief after which he entered non-league football playing for a number of clubs including Nuneaton Borough and Kidderminster Harriers.

JENKYNS, CAESAR Welsh international centre-half Caesar Jenkyns began his career playing for several Birmingham youth sides before joining the Blues as a professional in the summer of 1888. He led the club to the Second Division championship in 1892–93 only for them to lose the Test match series. However, the following season he was captain when the Blues gained promotion. He had scored 13 goals in 99 league and cup games when in April 1895 he was transferred to Woolwich Arsenal. His name will remain in the Arsenal record book for all time, because in 1895–96 he became the club's first-ever current international. The Gunners, however, could not hold on to their prized asset and in May 1896 he joined Newton Heath. He spent two seasons with the Heathens, helping them win promotion to the First Division in 1897–98. He later played for Walsall before ending his professional career with Coventry.

JENNINGS, DENNIS One of the club's most versatile players, Dennis Jennings played in every position except centre-half in his 15-year association with the Blues. He began his Football League career with Huddersfield Town, whom he joined from Kidderminster Harriers before transferring to Grimsby Town in the summer of 1932. He helped the Mariners win the Second Division Championship in 1933–34 but left Blundell Park in January 1936 after scoring 29 goals in 102 games. He made his league début in a 1–0 defeat at home to Manchester City before scoring his first goal for the club in his next appearance as the Blues beat Blackburn Rovers 4–2. By the time the Second World War had started, Jennings had become the club's regular penalty-taker and in 1938–39, out of the seven goals he scored, five of them were from the spot. During the war, the man who played in 166 matches won a League South Championship medal in 1945–46. He won a Second Division Championship medal in 1947–48 but two seasons later he left the club after scoring 14 goals in 214 league and cup games, later becoming player-coach at Kidderminster.

JOHNSON, MICHAEL Michael Johnson had made 136 league and cup appearances for Notts County when he joined Birmingham City for a fee of £225,000 in September 1995. He made his début in a 5–0 win at Barnsley and went on to appear in 43 games in that 1995–96 season. Predominantly a left-sided player, it was thought at one stage that he would be surplus to requirements with Ablett, Breen and Bruce on the club's books but 'Magic', as he is nicknamed, continued to impress. His outstanding man-marking ability coupled with his impressive aerial ability have made the versatile Johnson one of the best defenders outside the Premier League. On 22 February 1998 he scored his first-ever league goal in a 2–0 win over Sheffield United and followed it up with a second a week later. The athletic City defender has, at the time of writing, appeared in 127 league and cup games for the club.

JONES, BILLY Known as the 'Tipton Slasher', Billy Jones joined the Blues from Halesowen in the summer of 1901 and played his first game for the club against Sheffield United on 19 October 1901, scoring in a 5–1 home win. After helping the club win promotion to the First Division in 1902–03, Jones established himself in the Blues' side, forming a good understanding with Benny Green. In 1904–05 he was the club's leading scorer with 16 goals in 30 games, a feat he repeated the following season with 24 goals in 41 games. The all-action centre-forward headed the charts for a third consecutive season in 1906–07 with 15 goals in 39 games. During those three seasons, he netted 12 'doubles' but always found the hat-trick elusive. When Jack Hall forced his way into the Birmingham side, Jones switched to inside-forward but was allowed to leave and join Brighton after suffering a series of injuries. After two seasons on the south coast, he returned to St Andrew's when the Blues were back in the Second Division. He was the club's leading scorer in 1912–13 with 16 goals in 34 games as the Blues finished third in Division Two. At the end of that season, however, after scoring 102 goals in 252 games, he rejoined Brighton, to later become the club's assistant-trainer.

JONES, CHARLIE After unsuccessful trials for both Blackburn Rovers and Bolton Wanderers, Charlie Jones signed professional forms for his local side, Wrexham. During two seasons at the Racecourse Ground he only made seven league appearances, spending most of his time playing centre-forward for the Welsh club's reserve side. In September 1934, Jones joined the Blues for a fee of £1,500 and made his début in a 2–0 defeat at Stoke. He went on to become the club's leading scorer with 17 goals in 28 games including a hat-trick in a 3–2 home win over Derby County. His form was such that in March 1935 he won the first of two full caps for Wales when he scored in a 1–1 draw against Scotland at Ninian Park. He topped Birmingham's scoring charts again in 1935–36 with 20 goals in 41 games, netting another hat-trick in a 4–1 defeat of Sheffield Wednesday at St Andrew's. Though he wasn't as prolific in the years leading up to the outbreak of the Second World War, he scored another hat-trick for the Blues in the 4–1 home win over Leicester City. During the early part of the hostilities, he 'guested' for Blackpool and scored 42 goals in 42 games before returning to St Andrew's to help

Birmingham win the League South Championship in 1945–46. He scored four goals in the opening two games of the 1946–47 season as the Blues returned to Football League action, but in September 1947 he left the club after scoring 71 goals in 151 league and cup games to join Nottingham Forest. After just seven league appearances for the City Ground club, in which he scored five goals, he left to play non-league football for Redditch United, later turning out for Kidderminster Harriers.

JONES, JACK Full-back Jack Jones began his career with Maltby FC before signing professional forms for Sunderland. Unable to break into the first team at Roker Park, he joined Birmingham in the summer of 1920 for a fee of £2,000. He made his début playing at right-back in a 5–1 home win over Hull City in the second game of the 1920–21 season, but soon switched to the left-back berth to accommodate Frank Womack. Strong in the tackle, 'Cracker' Jones was a full-back that opposition wingers feared. The Rotherham-born player always turned out in dentures until they were smashed on a close season tour to Spain when he took a full-blooded shot in the face – unbelievably, a penalty was awarded for handball against him! He went on to play in 237 league and cup games for Birmingham with his only goal for the club coming in a 2–1 home win over Manchester United in April 1926. At the end of the 1926–27 season, he left the club to play for Nelson before ending his league career with Crewe Alexandra.

JUBILEE FUND The League Benevolent Fund was launched in 1938, fifty years after the start of the Football League, to benefit players who had fallen on hard times. It was decided that the best way to raise funds was for sides to play local 'derby' games with no account being taken of league status. The Blues played Coventry City at Highfield Road as a pre-season friendly prior to the start of the 1938–39 and 1939–40 seasons, losing both games 2–0 and 3–2 respectively. In the second game the Blues did well, for they had lost the services of both Jones and Morris who were carried off injured.

K

KENDALL, HOWARD Howard Kendall, at 20 days before his eighteenth birthday, became the youngest player ever to appear in an FA Cup final when he played left-half for Preston North End against West Ham United in 1964. After making 104 appearances for the Deepdale club he joined Everton for £80,000 in March 1967 and in seven seasons at Goodison Park went on to be part of the most influential midfield combination the Toffees have ever had. He went on to play in 274 games for the club before joining Birmingham City in February 1974 as part of a complicated deal which took Bob Latchford to Everton. His first game for the St Andrew's club was in the local derby at Molineux which Wolves won 1–0. After that he quickly settled into the club's midfield and helped them establish themselves as a top-flight club. He also played in the 1975 FA Cup semi-final for the Blues when they lost 1–0 to Fulham in a replay, but in 1977 after scoring 18 goals in 134 games, he was transferred to Stoke City. After two seasons at the Victoria Ground he became player-manager at Blackburn Rovers and, after taking the Ewood Park club from the Third Division to the brink of the First Division, he was ready for the big time. On 8 May 1981 he returned to Goodison Park as Everton manager and led the Merseyside club to the League Championship, FA Cup glory and European Cup Winners' Cup success. Feeling he could do no more, he left to take charge of Atletico Bilbao. After two happy years he left by mutual consent and returned to England to manage Manchester City. He had been in charge at Maine Road for less than 12 months when he made the sensational move of resigning to return to Goodison. He stayed with the club until December 1993 when he quit after watching his side gain their first Premiership victory at home for ten weeks. He had spells in charge of Notts County and Sheffield United before becoming manager of Everton for a third time in

THE ST ANDREW'S ENCYCLOPEDIA

Howard Kendall

June 1997. At the end of the 1997–98 season he parted company again following a campaign in which the club hung on to their

Premiership status on goal difference from Bolton Wanderers.

KINSEY, NOEL Born in Treorchy on Christmas Eve 1925, he played in a couple of wartime games for Cardiff City after his goalscoring feats for Treorchy Amateurs had alerted the Ninian Park club. Surprisingly though, they didn't pursue their interest and in the summer of 1947 he joined Norwich City. Always alert around the penalty area, he top scored for the Canaries in 1949–50 with 17 goals in 42 league and cup games including eight in the first seven games of the season. He reached double figures in the next two seasons as the Carrow Road club finished second and third respectively in the Third Division (South). He had scored 65 goals in 243 games for Norwich when in the summer of 1953 he was allowed to join Birmingham City. In his second season at St Andrew's, he won a Second Division Championship medal, scoring 13 goals in 35 league games, and in 1956 he netted the Blues' goal in the 3–1 FA Cup final defeat against Manchester City at Wembley. He had been capped four times whilst with the Canaries but added another three caps to his collection whilst at St Andrew's where, after scoring 56 goals in 174 games, he joined Port Vale. After being a regular in the club's Fourth Division Championship side of 1958–59, he was appointed player-coach. On leaving Vale Park he had a short spell with King's Lynn before becoming a successful player-coach to Lowestoft Town.

KNIGHTON, LESLIE Leslie Knighton played the game at non-league level until an ankle injury ended his career. In 1904 whilst only 20, he took up his first managerial post with Castleford Town before being appointed five years later as assistant-secretary of Huddersfield Town. He later held a similar position with Manchester City before becoming secretary–manager of Arsenal in May 1919. He was not in complete control at Arsenal, where the club was in debt after moving to Highbury. The Gunners' chairman, Sir Henry Norris, instructed Knighton to build a successful side without spending any money. This, of course, was unrealistic and in six seasons with the Gunners he saw the club narrowly avoid relegation twice. In 1925, after a number of rows with Norris, he was sacked. He then took charge of Third Division Bournemouth but after three years at Dean Court, he moved to St Andrew's to become manager of Birmingham City. In his first two seasons with the club, the Blues finished 15th and 11th respectively, but in 1931 he led Birmingham to the FA Cup final where they lost 2–1 to West Bromwich Albion. The club finished ninth and 13th in the following two seasons but in the summer of 1933, Knighton left to manage Chelsea after they made him an offer he could not refuse. In his first season in charge at Stamford Bridge, the Pensioners had an amazing run to avoid relegation – as they did, in 1938–39 – but after six years in the post, he left to manage Midland League club Shrewsbury Town before ill-health forced him to retire.

KUHL, MARTIN After joining Birmingham City as an apprentice, Martin Kuhl worked his way through the ranks before making his first-team début in a 2–0 defeat at West Bromwich Albion in March 1983. His other appearance in that season came in the final game at Southampton which the Blues won 1–0. A versatile performer, he wore six different numbered shirts in 1983–84 and scored his first goal for the club in a 1–1 home draw against Arsenal. Following the Blues' relegation at the end of that campaign, Kuhl was instrumental in the St Andrew's club returning to the top flight at the first attempt, but after they lost their First Division status after just one season, he became unsettled and wanted a transfer. He had played in 134 games for the Blues when he joined Sheffield United in March 1987. A year later he left the Blades to play for Watford. Unable to settle at Vicarage Road he signed for Portsmouth and in four years at Fratton Park, scored 28 goals in 184 games before leaving to join Derby County for £650,000 in September 1992. He appeared in 84 games for the Rams before a short loan spell at Notts County. He later signed for Bristol City for £300,000 and soon settled down to demonstrate his capabilities. Having been voted Player of the Year in his first season at Ashton Gate, he has now appeared in 114 first-team games for the Robins.

L

LANE, JOE Born in Hereford in July 1892, Joe Lane joined Watford as an amateur in 1906 and then played in Hungarian football before signing for Sunderland in 1912. He left the Wearsiders in November 1913 to join Blackpool and scored on his début against Leeds City. After scoring another 10 goals in that 1913–14 season, it became obvious that Lane was a player of considerable skill. In 1914–15 he scored 28 goals in 39 games including hat-tricks against Hull City (Away 3–1) and Glossop (Home 3–0). During the war, Lane served in Egypt with the Hertfordshire Yeomanry before returning to help the Seasiders finish fourth in Division Two with 28 goals in 38 games including another hat-trick in a 6–0 home win over Lincoln City. He joined Birmingham for a club record fee of £3,600 in March 1920 and scored from the penalty-spot on his début in a 2–2 draw at Lincoln. He then scored two goals in his next game as Nottingham Forest were beaten 8–0 and then netted his first hat-trick for the Blues as Lincoln were beaten 7–0. His goals in 1920–21 helped the club win the Second Division Championship but then midway through the following season he left St Andrew's, having scored 26 goals in 67 games, to play for Millwall. After two seasons at The Den, he retired to become coach of Barcelona.

LANGAN, DAVID Dublin-born full-back David Langan joined Derby County straight from school and after a number of impressive performances in the club's Central League side, he was given his Football League début against Leeds United during the 1976–77 season. Langan became unsettled when the Rams (under Colin Addison) looked likely to be relegated. He refused to travel with the team to Bristol City in 1980 but then when he did turn up he was sent home and fined. In an attempt to ease Derby's

THE ST ANDREW'S ENCYCLOPEDIA

David Langan

financial situation, Langan was sold to Birmingham City for £350,000. Manager Jim Smith gave him his début in a 3-1 home win over Coventry City on the opening day of the 1980-81 season. After two reasonably successful years with the Blues, his career collapsed: a knee injury began his troubles and he was on crutches after his fourth operation when he fell and cracked a vertebra. He missed all the 1983–84 season and after 102 appearances, City manager Ron Saunders gave him a free transfer. Former Blues' manager Jim Smith signed him for Oxford United. Langan not only proved his fitness but helped the Manor Ground club win promotion to the First Division in 1985 and win the Football League Cup in 1986. The Republic of Ireland international, who won 25 full caps for his country, appeared in 114 league games for Oxford United before following a loan spell with Leicester City. After that he played for Bournemouth and then Peterborough United.

LARGEST CROWD It was on 11 February 1939 that St Andrew's housed its largest crowd. The occasion was the FA Cup fifth-round match against Everton. A staggering crowd of 66,844 saw Owen Madden score both Birmingham's goals in a 2–2 draw.

LATCHFORD, BOB A big, bustling centre-forward, Bob Latchford played his first game for the Blues against Preston North End in March 1969, scoring twice in a 3–1 win. A few months later he was playing for England in the International Youth Tournament in East Germany. It was 1970–71 before he won a regular place in the Blues' side and the following season he was ever present as the club won the Second Division Championship. Latchford top-scored with 30 goals – 23 of them in the league – including hat-tricks in the wins over Charlton Athletic (Home 4–1) and Watford (Home 4–1). Playing well alongside Trevor Francis and Bob Hatton, he continued to find the net in the top flight, scoring 19 league goals along with another hat-trick in a 4–1 home win over Manchester City. He had scored 84 goals in 194 games for the Blues when in February 1974 he joined Everton for £350,000. In his first four full seasons with the Goodison club, Latchford was the top league goalscorer, reaching his peak in 1977–78 when he became the first Division One player for six years to reach the 30-goal mark. Latchford reached the final game of that season at home to Chelsea, needing two goals to claim a national newspaper prize of £10,000. Everton won 6–0 and Latchford netted the goals necessary to win the money and carve a place for himself in Merseyside folklore. Latchford, who won 12 full caps for England, left Everton after scoring 138 goals in 289 league and cup games to join Swansea for £125,000. He scored a

Bob Latchford

hat-trick on his début in a 5–1 win over Leeds United but, after being given a free transfer, joined Dutch club, Breda. Within five months he had returned to England and signed for Coventry City. Twelve months later he left to play for Lincoln City before ending his league career with Newport County.

Dave Latchford

LATCHFORD, DAVE Goalkeeper Dave Latchford, elder brother of England international Bob, made his league début for the Blues in a 2–1 win at Bury in April 1969. During his first few years with the club he faced stiff opposition from Herriot, Cooper and Sprake and, though he played in 11 games during the Blues' promotion-winning season of 1971–72, it was the following season before he established himself as the club's first-choice keeper. Over the next five seasons, Latchford missed very few games and turned in a number of outstanding performances between the posts as the club struggled to avoid relegation from the First Division. He had appeared in 239 league and cup games for the Blues before losing his place to Jim Montgomery. After a spell with Scottish League side Motherwell, he signed for Bury where he played in just two league games before joining Barnsley as a non-contract player. He later played non-league football for Redditch United and Cheltenham Town.

LATE FINISHES Birmingham's final match of the season against Newport County at Somerton Park on 26 May 1947 is the latest date for the finish of any Blues season. During the war many curious things occurred, among them the continuance of the 1939–40 season into June. Thus the Blues' last competitive match in that campaign was on 8 June when goals from Bodle(2), Duckhouse(2), Jones(2), Brown and a Godfrey own-goal gave them an 8–1 home win over Walsall.

LEADING GOALSCORERS The Blues have provided the Football League's leading divisional goalscorer on two occasions:

Season	Player	Division	Goals
1905–06	Bullet Jones	Football League	26
1971–72	Bob Latchford	Division Two	23

LEAGUE GOALS – CAREER HIGHEST Joe Bradford holds the St Andrew's record for the most league goals with a career total of 249 goals between 1920 and 1935.

LEAGUE GOALS – LEAST CONCEDED During the 1947–48 season, the Blues conceded just 24 goals in 42 games when winning the Second Division Championship. The club also conceded 24 goals in 1900–01 when finishing runners-up in the Second Division but that was in a 34-match programme.

LEAGUE GOALS – MOST INDIVIDUAL Walter Abbott holds the Birmingham record for the most league goals scored in a season with 34 scored in the Second Division during the 1898–99 season.

LEAGUE GOALS – MOST SCORED Birmingham's highest goals tally in the Football League was during the 1893–94 season when they scored 103 goals and finished runners-up in the Second Division.

LEAGUE VICTORY – HIGHEST The Blues' best league victory is 12–0, a scoreline achieved in two games. The first occasion was on 17 December 1892 when they beat Walsall Town Swifts at Muntz Street. Billy Walton and Fred Mobley both scored hat-tricks whilst Freddie Wheldon, Jack Hallam and Tommy Hands netted two goals apiece. The Blues then repeated the feat on 11 April 1903 against Doncaster Rovers, a match in which both Arthur Leonard and Freddie Wilcox scored four goals apiece.

LEAKE, ALEX Alex Leake began his career with King's Heath Albion, moving to Old Hill Wanderers in 1892 before joining the Blues two years later. He made his début playing at left-half in a 3–2 defeat at Preston North End, but soon switched to centre-half where he proved himself to be a natural defender. An ever-present in 1898–99, he helped the club win promotion to the First Division two seasons later but in the summer of 1902, after scoring 23 goals in 221 games, he left to join Aston Villa. He was an important member of Villa's FA Cup-winning side of 1905 and won the first of five full caps for England in 1904 in a 1–0 win over Scotland at Celtic Park. He appeared in 141 league and cup games for Villa before leaving to play for Burnley in December 1907. He had three years at Turf Moor before signing for Wednesbury Old Athletic. In 1912 he joined Crystal Palace as trainer and despite being 40 years of age, he was selected as England's reserve. After the hostilities he was appointed trainer at Merthyr Town before he went on to coach at schools and colleges around Britain.

LEEK, KEN Welsh international centre-forward Ken Leek, who once scored twice in the last three minutes in a 3–2 win over Scotland, began his Football League career with Northampton Town and had scored 29 goals in 77 games for the Cobblers when in May 1958 he left the County Ground to join Leicester City. The hard-working forward continued to find the net for the Filbert Street club so that he had, in fact, scored in every round during the Foxes run to the 1961 FA Cup final. On the morning of the match against 'double' chasing Tottenham Hotspur, however, he was dropped. Not surprisingly, he left Leicester in the summer after having scored 34 goals in 93 league games to join Newcastle United. Unable to settle at St James Park, he joined Birmingham City in November 1961 and made his début for the Blues in a 3–1 defeat at Sheffield United. Though he only played in 24 games that season, he was the club's top scorer with 18 goals including a spell of 12 goals in 12 games. In 1962–63 he again headed the club's goalscoring charts with 30 league and cup goals including two in the first leg of the League Cup final when the Blues beat Aston Villa 3–1. After scoring 61 goals in 120 games for the St Andrew's club, he returned to Northampton Town where he took his tally of goals to 33 in 93 games before signing for Bradford City. On leaving Valley Parade, he played non-league football for Rhyl Town and Ton Pentre before hanging up his boots.

LESLIE, ALEC Wing-half Alec Leslie played his early football with Houghton-le-Spring but his big chance came when he returned to his native Scotland to play for Morton in the Scottish First Division. He later played for St Mirren before joining Torquay United. The Blues paid the Plainmoor club £750 for Leslie's services in March 1927 and he went straight into the club's league side for the game at Leeds United which the Yorkshire club won 2–1. After that, Leslie was a virtual ever-present in the Birmingham side for the next five seasons, appearing in all the games of the 1927–28 campaign. Towards the end of the 1929–30 season his progress was interrupted by injuries and, though he bounced back to become an important member of the Blues' side that reached the FA Cup final in 1931, a recurring knee injury forced his retirement from the game after he had made 143 first-team appearances for the St Andrew's club.

LEYLAND DAF CUP A competition designed solely and specifically for Associate Members of the Football League, the Leyland Daf Cup replaced the Sherpa Van Trophy for the 1989–90 season. Birmingham's first game in the competition was a 3–0 defeat at Aldershot and, though an Ian Atkins goal gave them victory against Hereford United in their other preliminary-round match, they failed to qualify for the knockout stages. In 1990–91, the Blues won both of their preliminary-round games, beating Walsall (Away 1–0) and Lincoln City (Home 2–0). In the first round City were held at home to a goalless draw by Swansea but then won 4–2 on penalties. In the Southern Area quarter-final, goals from Matthewson and Gayle gave them a 2–0 victory over Mansfield Town to set up the Area semi-final against Cambridge United at St Andrew's. After a comfortable 3–1 win, the Blues met Brentford in the Southern Area final over two legs. Goals from Rodgerson and Gayle gave the Blues a 2–1 first-leg lead to take to Griffin Park for the second match. With strong support in the 8,745 crowd, City won 1–0 thanks to a Simon Sturridge goal. In the final at Wembley in front of a crowd of 58,756, City took the lead against Tranmere Rovers after 21 minutes when Simon Sturridge scored with an opportunist goal. Then, just before half-time, the Blues extended their lead when John Gayle cracked home a 30-yard drive. Tranmere goalkeeper Eric Nixon made a breathtaking save on the stroke of half-time, otherwise the game would have been out of Tranmere's reach. In the second-half, the Prenton Park club pushed forward and after Steve Cooper had reduced the arrears, Jim Steel levelled the scores after 66 minutes. The game could have gone either way but with just four minutes remaining, John Gayle – with his back to goal – scored the winner after producing a remarkable scissor-kick that sent the ball into the top corner of the net.

LIDDELL, GEORGE George Liddell made his début for the Blues in a 3–0 defeat at his former club South Shields on the opening day of the 1920–21 season. Though he turned out at wing-half on a number of occasions over the next three seasons, it was 1924–25 before he established himself as a first-team regular. However, towards the end of the 1927–28 season, Liddell was tried at right-back where his strong tackling and good distribution stood him in good stead. He captained the club on a number of occasions and he appeared for the Blues in the FA Cup final of 1931 against West Bromwich Albion. He went on to play in 345 league and cup games for Birmingham before being appointed the club's manager in July 1933 following the departure of Leslie Knighton. Despite inheriting a fine squad of players, Liddell failed to bring success to the club during his six years as manager. In fact, after coming close to losing their First Division status on a number of occasions, the Blues were relegated to the Second Division in 1938–39.

LOWEST The lowest number of goals scored by the Blues in a single league season is 30 in 1985–86 when the club finished 21st in Division One and were relegated. The club's lowest points total in the League occurred in 1895–96 when the Blues gained just 20 points and were relegated to Division Two.

LYNN, STAN Bolton-born full-back Stan Lynn began his career with Accrington Stanley whom he joined as a professional from Whitworths FC in the summer of 1947. He had appeared in 25 league games when Aston Villa paid £10,000 for his services in March 1950. After making his Villa début at left-back he switched to right-back, forming a fine full-back partnership with Peter Aldis. Lynn was Villa's first-choice right-back for seven seasons after establishing himself on the side in 1954. He helped Villa win the FA Cup in 1957, the Second Division Championship in 1960 and played in the first leg of the 1961 League Cup final. In January 1958 he became the first full-back to score a hat-trick in a Division One game as Villa beat Sunderland. He had scored 38 goals in 323 games, the majority from free-kicks or penalties, when he left to join Birmingham City in October 1961 for £15,000. He made his début for the Blues in a 3–2 home win over Chelsea and went on to give the club four seasons good service before losing his place to Cammie Fraser. In 1963 he won another League Cup winners' award when City beat Villa. He scored 30 goals in 148 games for the Blues before leaving to play non-league football for Stourbridge.

M

McCLURE, ALEX Alex McClure began his career with Grangetown before moving to the West Midlands where he was to make his home. He joined the Blues in the summer of 1911 and made his début in a 2–0 home win over Stockport County in January 1912. In the years leading up to the outbreak of the First World War, McClure was in and out of the Birmingham side and indeed captained the club's reserve side to victory in three competitions in the same season. He was a sailor in the war and participated in the Zeebrugge Affair, one of the great military actions of World War One. When league football resumed in 1919–20, McClure was the club's first-choice centre-half. He led the Blues to the Second Division title in 1920–21 and, despite a series of injuries, represented the Football League on two occasions. In December 1923, after having scored four goals in 198 league and cup games, he joined Aston Villa. Within a year, however, he had moved to play for Stoke. He later had spells with Coventry City and Walsall and was trainer to Luton Town before Birmingham manager Leslie Knighton tempted him back to St Andrew's as his assistant-manager in 1928. The McClure family had strong links with football. His brother Sammy was at Blackburn and his nephew, Joe, at Everton. After finishing at St Andrew's, he worked at Rudge Motorcycles and then ran a haulage firm at Small Heath.

McROBERTS, BOB Scottish centre-forward Bob McRoberts played for both Airdrieonians and Albion Rovers before joining Gainsborough Trinity in the summer of 1896. After two seasons he moved to play for the Blues and made his début in the opening game of the 1898–99 season, when he scored twice in a 6–2 win at Burton Swifts. That season saw him score his first hat-trick for the club in a 10–0 FA Cup win against the Druids. The following season, McRoberts was the club's leading scorer with 24 goals, a total which included hat-tricks against his former club Gainsborough Trinity (Home 8–1), Middlesbrough (Away 3–1), Lincoln City (Home 5–0) and Wrexham in the FA Cup (Home 6–1). In March 1901, McRoberts scored five of Birmingham's goals in a 10–1 home win over Blackpool and continued to score on a regular basis until the end of the 1904–05 season when he left St Andrew's to join Chelsea. McRoberts, who had scored 82 goals in 187 games for the Blues, switched to play centre-half for the Stamford Bridge club and captained them in the majority of his 106 appearances before hanging up his boots. After a year out of the game, he was appointed Birmingham's first full-time manager in the summer of 1910. After engaging former Villa and England goalkeeper Billy George as his assistant, McRoberts was in charge for five seasons up to the outbreak of the First World War when, in 1914–15, they finished fifth in the Second Division, their best position under his leadership. McRoberts then retired and though the board tried to persuade him to return to the club after the hostilities, he decided against it.

MACARI, LOU After finding it all too easy to win honours with Celtic, Lou Macari moved south of the border to Old Trafford for a new challenge. He helped United back into the First Division and appeared in three FA Cup finals, collecting a winners' medal in 1977. After scoring 88 goals in 391 games for United, he joined Swindon Town as player–manager. He was sacked in April 1985 after a row with his assistant Harry Gregg but was reinstated six days later and he went on to steer the club from the Fourth to the Second Division in two seasons. In July 1989 he took over at West Ham United but lasted just seven months at Upton Park because in January 1990 the FA charged Macari, along with Swindon chairman Brian Hillier, with unauthorised betting on a Swindon match. He returned to management with Birmingham City a year later but, despite taking the Blues to the Leyland Daf final where they beat Tranmere Rovers 3–2, he resigned shortly afterwards, saying the club lacked ambition! He then managed Stoke City and in 1992–93 led them to the Second Division title. In November 1993 he was offered the manager's job at Celtic but seven months later he was sacked. Within four months he was back at the Victoria Ground and left a second time in 1997.

MACKAY, DAVE Within months of making his début for Hearts, Dave Mackay was the proud possessor of a League Cup winners' medal as they beat Motherwell at a rain-swept Hampden Park in October 1954. Eighteen months later, Hearts won the Scottish Cup but the best was yet to come. In 1957–58 Hearts won the League Championship and Mackay, who was captain, was named Scotland's Player of the Year. He won his first cap for Scotland against Spain in Madrid in 1957. Although he went on to captain his country in only his third international, he had an erratic international career, which brought him just 22 caps in eight years! In March 1959, Spurs paid £30,000 for his services. Three FA Cup wins, a League Championship (including the coveted 'double' in 1961) and European Cup Winners' Cup triumph in nine unforgettable years at White Hart Lane provides the evidence of his greatness. A twice-fractured leg sidelined him for the best part of two years but when he returned to full fitness, the great Spurs' side of the early '60s was no more. However, his will to win was as strong as ever and in 1967 he helped Spurs win the FA Cup for the third time in seven seasons. In 1968 he joined Derby County and after helping the Rams win the League Championship, he was named Footballer of the Year for 1969 alongside Manchester City's Tony Book. After hanging up his boots, Mackay managed Derby County to the First Division title and also had spells in charge of Swindon Town, Nottingham Forest, Walsall and Doncaster Rovers before taking charge at St Andrew's in April 1989. Unfortunately he had a number of run-ins with the club's owners and in January 1991 he was sacked while the impoverished City struggled in the lower reaches of the Third Division.

MALLETT, JOE Gateshead-born half-back Joe Mallett began his career with Charlton Athletic in 1935 and made two league appearances before joining Queen's Park Rangers just before the outbreak of the Second World War. In February 1947, Southampton paid £5,000 for his services and he made his début in a 3–2 win at Plymouth Argyle, scoring the winning goal with just minutes remaining. He soon established himself in the Southampton side and over the next six seasons, played in 223 league and cup games, many of them as captain. At the end of the 1953–54 season he joined Leyton Orient before becoming coach at Nottingham Forest. He held that position until July 1964 when he was appointed manager of Birmingham City. Though he was a shrewd, unflappable man, nothing went right for him at St Andrew's. The Blues were relegated to the Second Division in his first season in charge and despite making a number of good signings, he was unable to turn things round. In December 1965, Stan Cullis was appointed as City's boss whilst Mallett was kept on as assistant-manager. Both men left the club in March 1970 and Mallett, after a short spell as Southampton coach, managed Greek side Panionois. He did a good job there but encountered a lot of problems when the military junta was overthrown. The colonels appointed managers in Greek clubs and Mallett was given a hard time after their downfall. He was even under arrest for a while!

MANAGERS This is the complete list of Birmingham's full-time managers with the dates inclusive during which they held office:

Bob McRoberts	1910–1915	Fred Goodwin	1970–1975
Bill Beer	1923–1927	Willie Bell	1975–1977
Leslie Knighton	1928–1933	Sir Alf Ramsey	1977–1978
George Liddell	1933–1939	Jim Smith	1978–1982
Willie Camkin	1939–1945	Ron Saunders	1982–1986
Ted Goodiert	1945	John Bond	1986–1987
Harry Storer	1945–1948	Gary Pendrey	1987–1989
Bob Brocklebank	1949–1954	Dave Mackay	1989–1990
Arthur Turner	1954–1958	Lou Macari	1991
Albert Beasley	1958–1960	Terry Cooper	1991–1994
Gil Merrick	1960–1964	Barry Fry	1994–1996
Joe Mallett	1964–1965	Trevor Francis	1996–
Stan Cullis	1965–1970		

MANGNALL, DAVE Dave Mangnall played his early football with Maltby New Church, for whom he scored 52 goals in one season and then followed that with 35 for Maltby Colliery. After trials with Rotherham United and Huddersfield Town, he played as an amateur with Doncaster Rovers before signing professional forms for Leeds United. On 25 September 1929, Mangnall scored 10 goals for Leeds in a Northern Midweek League game against Stockport County in a 13–0 win. Four days later he was given his league début but after scoring six times in nine consecutive appearances, he was allowed to join Huddersfield Town in

December 1929. He finished the 1931–32 season with 33 league goals but injuries interrupted his progress and he joined Birmingham in February 1934. His first game for the Blues was in a 1–0 defeat at Leeds United but on his home début the following week he scored the winner in a 2–1 defeat of Derby County. In 1934–35 he scored 11 goals in 27 league and cup outings including a hat-trick in a 5–4 defeat at Liverpool! After only 13 months at St Andrew's, he joined West Ham United, scoring 29 goals in 37 games for the Upton Park club. He then signed for Millwall and led their attack when the Lions reached the FA Cup semi-finals and won the Third Division (South) Championship. He later played for Queen's Park Rangers before the war interrupted his career. After the hostilities, he managed Queen's Park Rangers, taking the Loftus Road club to the Third Division (South) title in 1947–48.

MARATHON MATCHES The Blues have been involved in two FA Cup games and a League Cup game that have gone to four matches. The first occasion was the first-round tie against Manchester United in 1903–04. After drawing 1–1 at Bank Street, the Blues were held by the same scoreline in the replay at St Andrew's. The third meeting was held at Bramall Lane, where the game also ended 1–1 after extra-time. The fourth meeting at Manchester City's Hyde Road ground saw United win 3–1. In 1983–84 the Blues drew 2–2 at home to Notts County in the League Cup third round before following two goalless draws after extra-time. They won 3–1 at Meadow Lane with Robert Hopkins scoring twice. The third occasion was in 1984–85 when after a goalless draw against Norwich City at St Andrew's, a Billy Wright goal gave the Blues a 1–1 draw after extra-time at Carrow Road. Dave Geddis netted for Birmingham in the third meeting at St Andrew's but it still ended all square before the Canaries won the fourth meeting 1–0. The club have also been involved in a number of games that have gone to three meetings – Leicester City (FA Cup third round 1948–49), Tottenham Hotspur (FA Cup sixth round 1952–53), Nottingham Forest (FA Cup fifth round 1958–59), Luton Town (League Cup second round 1972–73) and Crystal Palace (League Cup third round 1991–92).

MARKSMEN – LEAGUE Birmingham's top league goalscorer is

Joe Bradford who struck 249 league goals during his 15 years at St Andrew's. Only three players have hit more than 100 league goals for the club:

1.	Joe Bradford	249	6.	Geoff Vowden	79
2.	Trevor Francis	118	7.	Eddie Brown	74
3.	Peter Murphy	107	8.	Johnny Crosbie	71
4.	Billy Jones	99	9.	Bob McRoberts	70
5.	George Briggs	98	10.	Bob Latchford	68

MARKSMEN – OVERALL Five players have hit a century of goals for the Blues. The club's top marksman is Joe Bradford. The Century Club consist of:

1. Joe Bradford   267
2. Trevor Francis   133
3. Peter Murphy   127
4. George Briggs   107
5. Billy Jones   102

MARTIN, RAY Full-back Ray Martin joined Aston Villa in 1960 but was released a year later. After a trial at St Andrew's, he signed apprentice forms for the Blues. He turned professional in May 1962 and remained with the club for 14 years, amassing 374 league and cup appearances – a total that would have been much greater if his career hadn't been interrupted by injuries and illness. He made his City début in a 2–1 win at Manchester United in January 1964 and went on to become one of the most popular players ever to wear a blue shirt. He was elected the club's Player of the Year in 1969–70 and 1970–71, the only player to have won the award in two successive seasons. When Freddie Goodwin was appointed manager in 1970, he immediately appointed Martin as captain and in 1971–72 he led the club to promotion. Martin's only goal for Birmingham came in April 1970 when the Blues lost 4–2 at home to Hull City. When he left St Andrew's in May 1976, he went to play for Portland Timbers in the NASL but his stay was brief.

MATCH OF THE DAY Birmingham City's first appearance on BBC's *Match of the Day* was on 28 December 1964 when they lost

2–1 at West Ham United with Brian Sharples scoring the City goal.

MATTHEWSON, TREVOR Sheffield-born defender Trevor Matthewson began his league career with his home-town club, Sheffield Wednesday, whom he joined as an apprentice in February 1981. After only a handful of appearances he was given a free transfer and joined Newport County. In September 1985, turning out 90 times for the Somerton Park club, he moved to Stockport County, again on a free transfer. After a similar number of appearances for the Edgeley Park side he joined Lincoln City for a fee of £13,000 but in the summer of 1989, after two seasons at Sincil Bank, the Blues paid £45,000 to take the reliable central defender to St Andrew's. He made his début in a 3–0 home win over Crewe Alexandra on the opening day of the 1989–90 season when he went on to become the club's only ever-present and saw them finish seventh in Division Three. He was ever present again in 1990–91 and also played his part in the club winning the Leyland Daf Cup final at Wembley. Matthewson spent four seasons at St Andrew's and had scored 13 goals in 203 games before leaving to join Preston North End in the summer of 1993. After just one season at Deepdale, he moved to Bury before leaving to play non-league football for Witton Albion. He later returned to league action with Hereford United.

MERRICK, GIL Goalkeeper Gil Merrick always modelled himself on his childhood favourite, Harry Hibbs. After playing his early football with Shirley Juniors and Solihull Town, he joined the Blues as a professional in the summer of 1939. Though the Second World War prevented him from making his league début, he did appear in 172 games for the Blues during the hostilities and helped the club win the League South Championship in 1945–46. He also 'guested' for a number of clubs including Nottingham Forest and West Bromwich Albion. He eventually made his Football League début in a 2–1 win at Spurs on the opening day of the 1946–47 season and missed just one game as the club finished third in Division Two. The following season he helped the club win the Second Division Championship and in 1951 won the first of 23 full caps for England when he played in a 2–0 win over Northern Ireland at Villa Park. At international level,

Merrick was on the losing side on only five occasions, two of which were heavy defeats against Hungary. He was Birmingham's first-choice keeper for 13 seasons and was an ever-present in 1949–50 and 1950–51 when he appeared in 126 consecutive league games. He helped the Blues win the Second Division Championship again in 1954–55 and played in the 1956 FA Cup final when they lost 3–1 to Manchester City. Merrick, who played his last game against Leeds United in October 1959, holds the club record for the number of first-team appearances in a City shirt: a total which reached 551. After retiring at the end of the 1959–60 season, he was appointed the Blue's team manager. Almost immediately he saw City lose to Barcelona in the second leg of the Inter Cities Fairs Cup final in Spain and remained in that country to study Spanish football methods and organisations. On his return to St Andrew's, the club's performances improved a little but they still ended the 1960–61 season in 19th place. After losing to AS Roma in the Fairs Cup final carried over from the previous season, the Blues finished 17th in the First Division. In fact, they were constantly fighting against relegation during Merrick's time in office but they did beat Aston Villa over two legs to win the 1963 League Cup final. He was sacked a year later after another season of struggle and became manager of Bromsgrove Rovers before taking charge at Atherstone Town.

MILLINGTON, CHARLIE Utility forward Charlie Millington played his early football with Grantham and Ripley Athletic before beginning his league career with Aston Villa. He had scored 14 goals in 38 games for Villa when in October 1907, he moved to Fulham for a fee of £400. Within a month of his arrival at Craven Cottage, he had scored four goals in a game against Glossop and went on to find the net 21 times in 63 games. He left the London club to sign for Birmingham and scored on his début in a 2–2 home draw against Oldham Athletic on the opening day of the 1909–10 season. Though never a prolific scorer, his speed on the wing created a number of opportunities for his team-mates. At the end of the 1911–12 season, however, and having scored 13 goals in 87 games, he left the club. Also a well-known amateur cricketer with Lincolnshire in the Minor Counties Championship, he went back to work as an iron moulder in a Lincoln factory.

MITCHELL, FRANK Australian-born Frank Mitchell had hoped to play Test cricket for the country of his birth but, after coming to England in his teens with his parents, he became a professional footballer. After joining Coventry as an amateur and playing in their Birmingham Combination side, he left to sign for the Blues in September 1943. He made his début for the St Andrew's club during the Second World War and 'guested' for a number of clubs including Arsenal, Northampton and Portsmouth. The classy wing-half helped the Blues reach the FA Cup semi-finals in 1945–46 and collected a League South Championship medal. He made his league début in a 2–1 win at Tottenham Hotspur on the opening day of the 1946–47 season. He missed just one match during that campaign as he did in 1947–48 when the club won the Second Division Championship. Mitchell, who had been a reserve for England on a few occasions, was also an expert penalty-taker and in 106 games he scored eight goals for the Blues. He left St Andrew's in January 1949 when he joined Chelsea. After 85 appearances for the Stamford Bridge club, he moved to Watford and played in 193 league games before retiring in 1958.

MOBLEY, FRANK Handsworth-born centre-forward Frank Mobley joined the Blues from Singers FC (Coventry) in April 1892. He scored on his début on 24 September 1892 as Lincoln City were beaten 4–1 at Muntz Street and went on to score 14 goals in 19 league games, helping the Blues to the Second Division Championship. However, it was 1893–94 when they won promotion to the top flight after beating Darwen in a Test match at the Victoria Ground. That campaign saw Mobley top score with 24 goals in 21 games including hat-tricks in a 5–2 win at Lincoln City and a 7–0 triumph at Northwich Victoria. He continued to find the net over the next two seasons and had taken his tally of goals to 64 in 103 league and cup games when he left the Blues to join Bury. Injuries forced his retirement, however, after just three league appearances for the Gigg Lane club.

MONTGOMERY, JIM Sunderland-born goalkeeper Jim Montgomery joined his home-town club on leaving school in 1958 and turned professional at Roker Park in October 1960. After making his league début in a 2–1 home win over Derby

Jim Montgomery

County in February 1962, he went on to become a permanent fixture for the next 16 seasons, though he missed much of 1964–65 due to a hand injury. He was ever present in five seasons, including 1963–64 when the club won promotion to the First Division. He won an FA Cup winners' medal in 1973, when his magnificent double save thwarted Leeds United. There is no doubt that Jim Montgomery was one of the best goalkeepers in the Football League during the 1960s and early 1970s and was unlucky not to have added a full cap to his England Youth and Under–23 honours. Montgomery went on to make 623 first-team appearances for the Wearsiders before joining Birmingham City on a free transfer in February 1977 after a loan spell at Southampton. He made his début in a goalless draw at Derby County and in 1977–78 missed just one game as the Blues finished eleventh in the First Division. He had played in 73 league and cup games for the St Andrew's club when he joined Nottingham Forest as cover for Peter Shilton. After a short spell as temporary coach at Birmingham, he returned to the north-east to become senior coach at Roker Park.

MORRALL, GEORGE George Morrall signed for Birmingham in March 1927 after an unsuccessful trial for West Bromwich Albion and made his league début for the Blues nine months later in a 4–1 defeat at Derby County. It was midway through the following season of 1928–29 that the giant centre-half won a regular place in the Blues' first team. Commanding in the air and with a crunching tackle, the Smethwick-born defender was on the verge of full England honours during the 1930–31 season when he was instrumental in the club reaching that season's FA Cup final. Morrall spent nine seasons at St Andrew's and played in 266 league and cup games before leaving the Blues in the summer of 1936 to join Swindon Town. He played in 98 games for the Wiltshire club before retiring during the Second World War.

MORRIS, HARRY Joining Small Heath in 1883, Harry Morris made his début in November 1884 in a 2–0 FA Cup defeat against Birmingham Excelsior. He played his first few matches for the club at centre-forward before later switching to right-half. He captained the club on numerous occasions but played in just one league game in February 1893 when the Blues beat Bootle 6–2 on their way to winning the Second Division Championship. In 1903 Morris joined the board of directors and three years later had the foresight to realise that the muddy, flooded former brickworks which lay off Garrison Lane, just down the road from the club's Muntz Street ground, had the potential to rival the area's other newly opened grounds at Villa Park and the Hawthorns. This was soon converted to the stadium which is now the Blues' home.

MOST MATCHES Birmingham City played their greatest number of matches, 65, in 1995–96. This comprised 46 League games, two FA Cup games, 12 League Cup games and five Anglo-Italian Cup games.

MULRANEY, AMBROSE Ambrose 'Jock' Mulraney began his career with Celtic but never really settled at Parkhead and, after trials with a number of clubs including Blackpool and Clapton Orient, he joined non-league Dartford. In 1936 he moved to Ipswich Town and after helping them win the Southern League Championship in his first season at Portman Road, he scored the club's first hat-trick in the Football League against Bristol City. During the Second World War, Mulraney 'guested' for several clubs including Blackburn Rovers, Chelsea, Manchester City and Wolves. He also 'guested' for the Blues, scoring 34 goals in 118 games until he joined the St Andrew's club on a permanent basis in 1945, costing the Blues £3,750. In 1945–46 he played in all of the club's 10 matches in their run to the FA Cup semi-finals and scored a hat-trick in a 5–0 home win over Watford in the first leg of the fourth round. That season also saw him win a League South Championship medal, scoring 13 goals in 38 games. He made his Football League début for the club in a 2–1 win at Spurs on the opening day of the 1946–47 season and went on to score nine goals in 31 games before leaving to play for Shrewsbury Town at the end of the season. After a brief spell with Kidderminster Harriers, he played for Aston Villa before ending his involvement with the game as player–manager of Brierley Hill.

MUNTZ STREET This was the club's third ground and though they played here for 29 years, it was not an ideal playing surface. In fact, it was so uneven and rutted that when Wednesbury Old Athletic were drawn to play a cup-tie there, they offered the home club £5 to reverse the venue! During their stay at Muntz Street, the club built only one small stand there and by the early 1900s it was obviously becoming inadequate in coping with the larger crowds. In February 1903, for the match against Aston Villa, an estimated crowd of 35,000 were inside the ground, though a good 5,000 had stormed the turnstiles and got in without paying. In view of the fact that the rent had risen to £300 a year and the landlord had refused to extend the lease beyond 1907 or sell the freehold, the club decided to look for a new ground. The last game played at Muntz Street was against Bury on 22 December 1906 which the Blues won 3–1.

MURPHY, PETER Inside-forward Peter Murphy was on Birmingham's books as an amateur before signing professional forms for Coventry City. After finishing the 1949–50 season as top scorer for the Sky Blues, he was signed by Tottenham Hotspur for £18,500 as the White Hart Lane club sought to strengthen a squad that had already won the Second Division title. He made a goalscoring début for Spurs in a 4–1 win at Bolton Wanderers and finished the season with nine goals in 25 games as the London club won the League Championship. However, he was unable to command a permanent place in the Spurs side, so when they agreed to transfer him to Birmingham City for £20,000, he jumped at the chance. Making his début at home to Doncaster Rovers on 19 January 1952, the Hartlepool-born forward scored a hat-trick in a 5–0 win for the Blues. In 1952–53 he set a new post-war goalscoring record for the St Andrew's club with 26 goals in 38 league and cup games including hat-tricks against Leicester City (Away 4–3) and Oldham Athletic (Away 3–1). When the Blues won the Second Division Championship in 1954–55, Murphy was the club's leading scorer with 20 league goals. The following season he was instrumental in helping the Blues reach the FA Cup final at Wembley, scoring in each of the four rounds up to the semi-final. In the final against Manchester City, he was involved in the accident in which opposing goalkeeper Bert Trautmann broke his neck. In 1957–58, Murphy was once again the club's leading scorer with 23 goals including another hat-trick in a 4–0 home win over Manchester City. He was a regular in the City side until the end of that season and when he finished his playing career in 1960, he had scored 127 goals in 278 first-team outings. He later had a spell on Coventry's coaching staff before going into the licensing trade where he worked as a representative for Davenport's Brewery.

MURRAY, BERT An England Schoolboy and Youth international, Bert Murray began his league career with Chelsea, where his early performances led to his winning six England Under-23 caps. He helped the club win the League Cup in 1965 but at the end of the following season, after scoring 44 goals in 183 games for the Stamford Bridge club, he signed for Birmingham for a fee of £25,000. He played his first game for the Blues on the opening day of the 1966–67 season, scoring both the club's goals in a 2–1 win at Wolverhampton Wanderers. He scored in the first three games of the season, in fact, as City beat Portsmouth 5–4 at Fratton Park and Norwich 2–1 in the first game at St Andrew's. Murray was able to play in a variety of positions – an orthodox winger, midfield and right-back, which is where he gave his best performances for the Blues. In the final game of the 1969–70 season, he scored his only hat-trick for the club as the Blues beat Queen's Park Rangers at home 3–0. He had scored 23 goals in 162 first-team outings when he was transferred to Brighton and Hove Albion in February 1971. He later ended his career with Peterborough United, having scored 96 goals in 517 league games for his four clubs.

N

NDLOVU, PETER A Zimbabwe international from the age of 15, Ndlovu was first spotted by Coventry City during their summer tour of that country in 1990. After being invited for a trial, he signed a contract the following summer. He made his league début for the Sky Blues at Queen's Park Rangers in August 1991. Despite all the travelling involved in representing Zimbabwe in African Nations Cup matches, Ndlovu has scored some brilliant goals – the highly talented striker or midfield player has amazing ball control and devastating pace. Sadly, his progress at Highfield Road was hampered by a knee injury picked up while on international duty with Zimbabwe in the summer of 1996. Two operations followed before he regained his place in the side but in July 1997, after scoring 41 goals in 196 games, he was allowed to join Birmingham City. Signed on a pay-as-you-play deal, the Zimbabwean international scored City's second goal in a 2–0 home win over Stoke on the opening day of the 1997–98 season. In fact, he scored four times in his first six games, before suffering a loss of form. He later returned to his best form and ended his first season at St Andrew's with 11 goals in 46 games.

NEAL, RICHARD Richard Neal began his career with Wolverhampton Wanderers, signing professional forms for the Molineux club after playing for the club's nursery side, Wath Wanderers. Unable to break into the first team, he joined Lincoln City but in April 1957, after scoring 11 goals in 115 league games for the Sincil Bank club, he signed for Birmingham City for a fee of £18,000 plus Albert Linnecar. He made his début for the Blues in a 2–0 home win over West Bromwich Albion and was a regular member of the City side for four seasons, during which time he missed very few matches. He was a member of the Birmingham side that played against Barcelona in the 1960 Inter Cities Fairs Cup final and the following season he captained the club. He had scored 18 goals in 197 games when he joined Middlesbrough after losing his place at wing-half to Terry Hennessey. He later returned to Lincoln City where he took his total of league appearances to 156 before playing non-league football for Rugby Town. In 1968 he moved into management, taking charge of Hednesford Town.

NEUTRAL GROUNDS Whilst St Andrew's has been used as a neutral ground for FA Cup semi-finals on nine occasions between 1907 and 1961, the Blues themselves have had to replay on a neutral ground in the FA Cup three times – Manchester United at Bramall Lane in 1903–04; Tottenham Hotspur at Molineux in 1952–53; and Nottingham Forest at Filbert Street in 1958–59. The club's involvement in the Test matches in seasons 1892–93 and 1893–94 were also played on neutral grounds. The club's FA Cup semi-finals were of course played on neutral grounds with the following results:

Date	Opponents	Venue	Score
06.03.1886	West Brom Albion	Aston Lower Ground	0–4
14.03.1931	Sunderland	Elland Road	2–0
23.03.1946	Derby County	Hillsborough	1–1
27.03.1946	Derby County	Maine Road	0–4
10.03.1951	Blackpool	Maine Road	0–0
14.03.1951	Blackpool	Goodison Park	1–2
17.03.1956	Sunderland	Hillsborough	3–0
23.03.1957	Manchester United	Hillsborough	0–2
27.04.1968	West Brom Albion	Villa Park	0–2
15.04.1972	Leeds United	Hillsborough	0–3
05.04.1975	Fulham	Hillsborough	1–1
09.04.1975	Fulam	Maine Road	0–1

Birmingham's FA Cup finals in 1931 and 1956, along with their appearances in the Leyland Daf and Auto Windscreen Shield finals at Wembley, also qualify for inclusion.

NEWCASTLE UNITED In 1973–74, Birmingham City met Newcastle United a record seven times – six games taking place in as many months:

Date	Competition	Venue	Result
22.10.1973	Texaco Cup	Home	Drew 1–1
30.10.1973	League Cup	Home	Drew 2–2
07.11.1973	League Cup	Away	Won 1–0
28.11.1973	Texaco Cup	Away	Drew 1–1*
05.12.1973	Texaco Cup	Away	Lost 1–3
08.12.1973	Division One	Home	Won 1–0
20.04.1974	Division One	Away	Drew 1–1

* Abandoned

Amazingly, the two clubs met another four times the following season – a total of 11 games in two seasons!

Date	Competition	Venue	Result
19.10.1974	Division One	Home	Won 3–0
23.10.1974	Texaco Cup	Away	Drew 1–1
06.11.1974	Texaco Cup	Home	Lost 1–4
26.04.1975	Division One	Away	Won 2–1

NEWMAN, JOHNNY Johnny Newman began his career with Birmingham City after winning Welsh international honours as a junior. Rated one of the club's better youngsters, he made his league début in a 3–1 home win over Coventry City in March 1952. In 1954–55, when the Blues won the Second Division Championship, Newman played in 17 games and was a member of the Birmingham side that lost to Manchester City in the 1956 FA Cup final. He had appeared in 65 league and cup games for the St Andrew's club when he was allowed to leave and join Leicester City in November 1957. After two years at Filbert Street, he moved to Plymouth Argyle who were seeking to strengthen a failing team. Able to fit into any defensive position, Newman stayed at Home Park for seven years and had appeared in 328 games when he left to become player–manager of Exeter City. He later became manager of the Grecians before taking charge of Grimsby Town. He took the Mariners out of the Fourth Division in 1978–79 before joining Derby County as Colin Addison's assistant. He then became manager at the Baseball Ground but was sacked after ten months in charge. He joined Hereford United as manager before becoming assistant-manager at Notts County.

NICKNAMES Birmingham's nickname is the Blues. Many players in the club's history have also been fondly known by their nicknames. They include:

Charlie Simms	1884–1893	Bowie
Johnny Crosbie	1920–1932	Peerless
George Briggs	1923–1933	Nippy
Ken Green	1947–1959	Slasher
Richard Neal	1957–1961	Ticker
Colin Withers	1961–1965	Tiny
Dave Robinson	1968–1973	Sugar
Wayne Clarke	1984–1987	Sniffer

NON-LEAGUE 'Non-League' is the shorthand term for clubs which are not members of the Football League. The Blues have a mixed record against non-league opposition in the FA Cup competition. The club's record since the First World War is:

Date	Opponents	Stage	Venue	Score
14.01.1928	Peterborough Utd	Round 3	Home	4–3
21.01.1939	Chelmesford City	Round 4	Home	6–0
03.01.1986	Altrincham	Round 3	Home	1–2
17.11.1990	Cheltenham Town	Round 1	Home	1–0
08.01.1994	Kidderminster. H.	Round 3	Home	1–2
12.11.1994	Slough Town*	Round 1	Away	4–0

*Played at St Andrew's

O

OLDEST PLAYER The oldest player to line-up in a Birmingham City team is Dennis Jennings. He was 40 years 190 days old when he played the last of his 212 first-team games for the club against Wolverhampton Wanderers (Away 1–6) on 6 May 1950.

OLLIS, BILLY Billy Ollis first came to Birmingham's attention when he impressed in friendly matches against them while playing for Warwickshire County. The tough-tackling right-half played his first game for the club in a 3–1 home win over Burton Swifts on the opening day of the 1891–92 Football Alliance season and ended the campaign as one of five ever-presents. In 1892–93, the club's first season in the Football League, Ollis was again ever present and scored his first goal for the club in a 6–2 home win over Northwich Victoria. That season the Blues won the Second Division Championship but were unable to claim a place in the top flight after losing in the Test matches. Ollis played in all the club's games in 1893–94 and again in 1894–95, the Blues' first season in the top flight. He took over the captaincy of the club when Caesar Jenkyns was sacked but held the post for only a short while before leaving to play for Hereford Thistle in February 1896. Ollis had played in 99 consecutive Football League games following his début, the last of which was a 7–2 defeat at the hands of Wolverhampton Wanderers.

ORRITT, BRYAN Born in the small Welsh village of Cwm-Y-Glo, Bryan Orritt was one of the few Welsh-speaking players in the Football League. At the age of 17 he was playing for Bangor in the Cheshire League and was twice chosen as a reserve for the Welsh international youth team. He turned professional with Birmingham City in January 1956, making his league début in a 1–1 draw at Leeds United in October 1956. Though he was able to play in a variety of positions, he found it difficult to hold down a regular place on the Blues' side. His best season for the club in terms of goals scored was 1957–58 when he netted 12 goals in 27 games. He played for Birmingham in the 1960 and 1961 Inter Cities Fairs Cup finals and won three Welsh Under-23 caps. Having scored 27 goals in 119 games, Orritt was transferred to Middlesbrough in March 1962 while serving a seven-day suspension following an incident during his play for Birmingham Reserves. Orritt was Middlesbrough's first playing substitute and during his time at Ayresome Park he played in all 11 positions. He had scored 23 goals in 128 games when he emigrated to South Africa to play for Johannesburg.

OVERSEAS PLAYERS Alberto Tarantini played in the 1978 World Cup final for Argentina against Holland before signing for the Blues from Boca Juniors. Capped 59 times by his country, he could not take to the English game and after 24 appearances his contract was cancelled. In 1981–82 manager Jim Smith signed two Dutchmen from Willem Tilburg – Bud Brocken and international Tony Van Mierlo – but after playing in 17 and 44 league games respectively, they left the club. Paul Peschisolido joined the Blues from Toronto Blizzards in November 1992 but, after scoring 17 goals in 48 games, he was transferred to Stoke City for £400,000. He returned to St Andrew's for a second spell before later playing for West Bromwich Albion and now Fulham. Pacy winger José Domínguez signed for Birmingham from Benfica for a fee of £180,000 in March 1994. He had only appeared in 35 games when he returned to Portugal to play for Sporting Lisbon for £1.8 million but he jumped at the chance to come back to England to play for Spurs. Swedish international Anders Limpar joined the Blues from Everton in January 1997 after having played previously for Arsenal, whom he joined from Cremonese. Unfortunately, Trevor Francis's signing only made five appearances before having his contract cancelled. The most recent overseas player to join the club was Tony Hey who signed from German side Fortuna Cologne during the 1997 close season. Other players with foreign sounding surnames include John Sleeuwenhoek, Ricky Sbragia, Martin Kuhl, Nicky Platnauer and Louie Donowa – all born in the British Isles!

OVERSON, VINCE A rugged central defender, Vince Overson began his Football League career with Burnley and soon became a commanding figure in the Clarets' defence. He helped the Turf Moor club win the Third Division Championship in 1981–82 before a series of injuries forced him to miss much of the following season. After the club was relegated to the Fourth Division in 1985, Overson refused the terms of a new contract and played for the whole of his last season at Turf Moor on weekly terms. He had appeared in 261 games for Burnley when in the summer of 1986 he joined his former boss John Bond at Birmingham City for a fee of £25,000. His first game for the Blues came in a 2–0 win at Stoke City on the opening day of the 1986–87 season. Over the next three seasons, Overson missed very few games for a struggling City side which was relegated to the Third Division in 1989. There was limited success to come in the League at St Andrew's but in May 1991 the Blues appeared at Wembley for the first time in 35 years in the final of the Leyland Daf Trophy. A crowd of 58,756 saw what proved to be the last of Overson's 213 appearances for the St Andrew's club, as Tranmere Rovers were beaten 3–2. Just weeks later he joined Stoke City for £55,000. The Potters reached the Third Division play-offs at the end of Overson's first season and a year later he captained them to the championship of the new Second Division. After playing in 216 games for Stoke he returned to Burnley on a free transfer where injuries have since hampered his career.

OWN GOALS Whilst a number of players have put through their own net playing for the Blues, perhaps one of the most unusual own goals was scored by Billy Edmunds in the dying seconds of the friendly match against Nechells, to give Birmingham's opponents a 4–3 win. It completed a five-minute 'hat-trick' for the club's first officially appointed captain!

P

PAGE, MALCOLM The club's most capped player – having appeared in 28 full international matches for Wales – Malcolm Page was a marvellous servant to the club, appearing in 394 games in 17 seasons at St Andrew's. The first of those appearances came in a 1–1 draw at Everton in February 1965 and between then and his last game at Brighton in September 1980, he played in every position except goalkeeper. He also proved his ability to play in a

Malcolm Page

variety of positions at international level, for after making his début against Finland in 1971, he turned out in four different positions for Wales. One of the club's greatest-ever players, he led the club to promotion to the First Division in 1971–72 and he appeared in three FA Cup semi-finals with the club. He left St Andrew's in February 1981 to join Oxford United after being rewarded with a testimonial six years earlier. He spent just one season at the Manor Ground before leaving the game to work as an insurance representative.

PENALTY SHOOT-OUTS Birmingham City were the first club to be involved in a penalty shoot-out in an FA Cup game. On 5 August 1972 at St Andrew's against Stoke City in a play-off for third place held over from the previous season, Birmingham won 4–3 after a goalless draw.

PENDREY, GARY Captain of the Blue's team that reached the FA Youth Cup final in 1967, he made his first-team début in a 1–0 home defeat against Crystal Palace in March 1969. At 18, Pendrey became the club's youngest-ever captain and though he was a first-team regular at full-back, centre-half or midfield for the next ten seasons, he missed a number of games through suspension. This was brought about because of his competitive approach to the game – in his testimonial year, he was sent off twice and charged with bringing the game into disrepute! He helped the club win promotion to the First Division in 1971–72 and to two FA Cup semi-finals. After appearing in 360 games he joined West Bromwich Albion before later playing for Torquay United and Bristol Rovers. In June 1982 he was appointed player–coach at Walsall but four years later was sacked along with manager Alan Buckley. In November 1986 he was appointed as assistant to Wolves' manager Graham Turner but in May 1987 he could not resist the chance to return to St Andrew's to become the club's manager. In his first season in charge, the Blues came very close to the relegation play-off position. Sadly, things went from bad to worse in his second season and at the end of the campaign, City were relegated to the Third Division for the first time in their history. Pendrey was offered a coaching role at the club but he refused and left St Andrew's on acrimonious terms.

Gary Pendrey

PICKERING, FRED Fred Pickering began his career as a full-back with Blackburn Rovers but Ewood Park club was well served in that department, and his opportunities were therefore somewhat limited. After some powerful displays at centre-forward in the club's reserve side, he was given a chance in that position in the first team. He had the happy knack of putting the ball in the net and after adding power and pace to his game, he began to create

Fred Pickering

a name for himself. In fact he became so prolific, scoring 59 goals in 123 league games for Rovers, that Everton manager Harry Catterick paid £85,000 to take Pickering to Goodison Park. He signalled his arrival on Merseyside with a hat-trick on his début in a 6–1 win over Nottingham Forest and two months later scored another hat-trick in his first match for England as the USA were beaten 10–0 in New York. Pickering enjoyed his best season with Everton in 1964–65 when he scored 37 goals in 51 league and cup games. When Everton reached the 1966 FA Cup final, Pickering, who missed the semi-final through injury, declared himself fit but Catterick had his doubts about his ability to last 90 minutes and did not select him for Wembley. His days on Merseyside were numbered and after scoring 68 goals in 107 outings, he joined Birmingham City for £50,000. He made his début in the opening game of 1967–68 as the Blues beat Bolton Wanderers 4–0 before going on to be one of only two ever-presents that season. Forming a good understanding with Barry Bridges and Geoff Vowden, he scored 15 goals in 50 games, though in 1968–69 he took his total for the club to 32 goals in 88 appearances. At the end of that season he returned to the north-west to play for Blackpool but after helping the Seasiders win promotion, he began a second spell with Blackburn Rovers before ending his league career with Brighton.

PITCH The St Andrew's pitch measures 115 yards x 75 yards.

PLASTIC Four Football League clubs have replaced their normal grass-playing pitches with artificial surfaces at some stage. Queen's Park Rangers were the first in 1981 but the Loftus Road pitch was discarded in 1988 in favour of a return to turf. Luton Town (1985), Oldham Athletic (1986) and Preston North End (1986) followed. The Blues have played on all four surfaces and although their record on plastic is not a good one, it is probably no worse than that of most clubs. City's first game on plastic was at Loftus Road on 19 November 1983 when they lost 2–1. The only other time they played at Queen's Park Rangers was two seasons later when they were beaten 3–1. The club's only game on the Kenilworth Road plastic of Luton Town was on 2 November 1985 when City lost 2–0. In 1986–87, the Blues secured their first point on plastic when goals from Whitton and an own goal by Linighan gave them a 2–2 draw at Oldham Athletic. The following season, goals from Frain and a Whitton penalty gave City a 2–1 win at Boundary Park, their first success on plastic, but in 1988–89 they came down to earth following a 4–0 defeat by the Latics. City's visits to Preston North End's Deepdale plastic resulted in a 2–2 draw and two defeats, 0–2 and 2–3.

PLAY-OFFS After finishing fourth in the First Division in 1998–99, the Blues played Watford over two legs but lost on penalties to the club that eventually won promotion to the Premier League.

POINTS Under the three-points-for-a-win system which was introduced in 1981–82, Birmingham City's best points tally was the 89 points in 1994–95 when they won the Endsleigh Insurance League Division Two. However, the club's best points haul under the old two-points-for-a-win system, was 59 in 1947–48 when they won the Second Division Championship. City's worst record under either system was the meagre 20 points secured in 1895–96 when they were relegated from Division One. That was, however, from a 30-match programme. The club's lowest points total from a 42-match season is 22 points in 1978–79 when the club finished 21st in the First Division and lost their top-flight status.

POSTPONED The bleak winter of 1962–63, described at the time as the 'Modern Ice Age', proved to be one of the most chaotic seasons in British soccer. The worst Saturday for League action in that awful winter was 9 February when only seven Football League fixtures went ahead. The worst Saturday for the FA Cup was 5 January, the day of the third round, when only three of the 32 ties could be played. Birmingham City v Bury had to be postponed 14 times and one futile attempt to play the game was abandoned. The tie was eventually played on 5 March 1963 with the sides drawing 3–3. The replay at Gigg Lane two days later saw the Shakers win 2–0.

PROMOTION The Blues have been promoted on 11 occasions. They were first promoted in 1893–94 when they had to take part in the Test matches after finishing runners-up in the Second Division. A 3–1 win over Darwen at Stoke's Victoria Ground took them into the First Division. The Blues were promoted a second time in 1900–01 as runners-up to Grimsby Town. While the defence conceded only 24 goals in 34 games, the forwards scored 57 goals including a 10–1 home win over Blackpool. After relegation in just one season, the Blues won promotion again in 1902–03, clinging on to the runners-up spot from Woolwich Arsenal. That season saw the Blues beat Doncaster Rovers 12–0. The Blue's fourth experience of promotion came in 1920–21 when they won the

Second Division Championship on goal average from Cardiff City. It was 1947–48 before the Blues won promotion again, winning the Second Division title with a new club defensive record of just 24 goals conceded over a 42-match programme. The club won the Second Division Championship again in 1954–55, beating runners-up Luton Town by 0.297 of a goal! The Blues won promotion for a seventh time in 1971–72 after being unbeaten in their last 18 games and winning their final game of the season 1–0 at Orient. Bob Latchford, who netted 23 league goals, was the scorer. The club won promotion again in 1979–80 when they finished third behind Leicester City and Sunderland. They needed a point from their final game of the season at home to Notts County and got it in a 3–3 draw. In 1984–85 the club won promotion at the first time of asking by finishing as runners-up to Oxford United, managed by former City boss Jim Smith. The Blues won promotion for a tenth time in 1991–92 when they ended the season as runners-up in the Third Division to Brentford. The club's last experience of promotion was in 1994–95 when they won the Second Division Championship after a run of 20 unbeaten league games.

PURDON, TED After touring England with the Maritz Brothers soccer team of Johannesburg, Ted Purdon was one of a number of South African players to be taken on at Birmingham City. Purdon had played his early football in Pretoria and joined the Maritz team in 1948. In a little over two years with the club, the tall blond striker had scored over 50 goals. He scored on his début for Birmingham on 29 August 1951 as City drew 1–1 at Leeds United. Though he never fully established himself in the first team in his three seasons at St Andrew's, he scored 30 goals in 70 first-team outings with a best of 15 in 23 league games in 1953–54. His last game for the Blues saw him score twice – his fifth double – in a 3–2 defeat at home to Rotherham United. In January 1954 he left St Andrew's and joined Sunderland, scoring twice on his début for the Wearsiders in a 5–0 win over Cardiff City. Then in his next match, he netted his only ever hat-trick in the top flight as Sunderland beat Arsenal 4–1 at Highbury. He went on to score 42 goals in 96 league and cup games for the north-east club before joining Workington. He later served Barrow, Bath City, Bristol Rovers and Toronto City before returning to his native South Africa where he became a successful businessman.

Q

QUICKEST GOAL The club's records do not include any precise goal times, so it is an impossible task to state accurately the club's quickest goalscorer. While there have obviously been quicker goals, James Higgins's 45-second goal in the FA Cup sixth-round tie against Manchester United helped the Blues into the 1951 semi-finals where they lost to Blackpool after a replay.

R

RAMSEY, SIR ALF As a player, Alf Ramsey was a strong, polished and distinguished defender who joined Portsmouth as an amateur in 1942. A year later he moved to The Dell to play for Southampton. He made his England début in a 6–0 victory over Switzerland at Highbury in December 1948 before going on to make 28 consecutive appearances for his country. In all, he won 32 caps for England and represented the Football League on five occasions. In May 1949 he moved to Tottenham Hotspur for £21,000, a record fee for a full-back. He was virtually an ever-present in the teams that won the Second Division and Football League titles in 1950 and 1951 and in May 1955, after appearing in 250 league and cup games for the White Hart Lane club, he retired. He was appointed manager of Ipswich Town in August 1955 and immediately began to refashion the Portman Road side in a manner which was to herald the dawn of a new era. He led the club to the Third Division (South) title in 1956–57, the Second Division Championship in 1960–61 and the First Division Championship in 1961–62. In January 1963 he was appointed the full-time manager of England. His greatest triumph came in 1966 when England, playing on home territory, won the World Cup for the first and only time. In May 1974, after England had failed to qualify for the finals of that year's World Cup competition, he was sacked. Under Ramsey, England only lost 17 out of 113 games and they won 69 of these. Shortly after the start of the 1977–78 season, Sir Alf Ramsey, who was by then a Birmingham City director, became the first knight to manage a League club following the dismissal of Willie Bell. He held office for seven months before being forced to relinquish the position due to ill-health.

RANSON, RAY Right-back Ray Ranson joined Manchester City as

Sir Alf Ramsey

an apprentice in the summer of 1976 and turned professional 12 months later. He made his league début for the Maine Road club in a goalless draw at home to Nottingham Forest in December 1978 and was a virtual ever-present for the next five seasons. He left Maine Road in November 1984 to join the Blues for a fee of £15,000 and played his first game for the club in a 2–1 defeat at Charlton Athletic. After two seasons, he began to be troubled by a series of niggling injuries and struggled to regain full fitness. Once he had, however, he produced a number of outstanding performances which, after playing in 157 games, led to his move to Newcastle United. He made 102 appearances for the Magpies before returning to Maine Road and taking his total appearances in his two spells with the club to 235. He later ended his league career with Reading before becoming player–manager of non-league Witton Albion.

RECEIPTS The club's record receipts are £230,000 for the League Cup second-round first-leg match against Aston Villa at St Andrew's on 21 September 1993.

RELEGATION The Blues have been relegated on 11 occasions. The club's first experience was in 1895–96 after just two seasons in the top flight. In fact, they were almost relegated at the end of their first-ever season in Division One but won 2–0 at Sheffield United on the last day of the season to prolong their stay of execution. The club were next relegated in 1901–02 but would have avoided the drop had they beat Notts County in their final game. Sadly they could only manage a goalless draw and went down with Manchester City. The club's third experience of relegation in 1907–08 saw them finish bottom of the table after losing their last game of the season 4–0 at home to Bristol City. In the final peacetime season of 1938–39 the Blues were undefeated in the final five games of the season but still went down with Leicester City. The Blues' lack of goals in 1949–50 when they could only score 31 cost them dearly, and after losing their final game of the season at Wolves 6–1, they finished bottom of the First Division and were relegated along with Manchester City. The Blues were next relegated in 1964–65 when they finished bottom of Division One and though they scored 10 goals in their last three games of the season, none of the matches were won and only two points taken! City were relegated again in 1978–79 which was Jim Smith's first season in charge. They failed to score in 17 of their games and only netted 37 goals with Alan Buckley top-scoring with eight. In the 1980s, the club suffered relegation on three further occasions – 1983–84, 1985–86 and 1988–89. After scoring just 39 goals in 1983–84, the Blues' shot-shy forwards could only hit the target 30 times in 1985–86. The Blues last suffered relegation in 1993–94 but thankfully won promotion to the First Division at the first attempt.

ROBB, BILLY Rutherglen-born goalkeeper Billy Robb played in local junior football in Lanarkshire before joining the Blues in the summer of 1912. He made his Football League début in a 3–1 defeat at Bury in February 1914 but only played in one further game that season. In 1914–15 Robb was the club's only ever-present as they finished sixth in Division Two, keeping 15 clean sheets in his 38 appearances. Sadly the First World War ended his association with Birmingham. In April 1920 he joined Glasgow Rangers and did not miss a game for the Ibrox Park club in five seasons with the Scottish side. He won four League Championship medals with Rangers and appeared in two Scottish Cup finals as well as winning two full caps, the first against Wales in 1926 and the second two years later when he joined Hibernian. After returning to the Football League with Aldershot, he finally ended his career with Guildford City, for whom he won a Southern League Championship medal.

ROBERTS, BRIAN Manchester-born 'Harry' Roberts was christened Brian but from his early days with his first club, Coventry City, he was given the nickname Harry after a notorious gangster from the late 1960s. A fine utility player, he hardly missed a game for the Sky Blues after establishing himself in the Highfield Road club's side in 1980–81 but, after appearing in 249 league and cup games, he left to join Birmingham City for £10,000. He made his début in a 2–1 defeat at Stoke City in March 1984 and the following season missed just one game as the Blues won promotion to the First Division. After six fairly traumatic years with Birmingham, in which he played in over 200 league and cup games, he moved to Wolverhampton Wanderers on a free transfer.

ROBERTS, JOHN John Roberts started his professional career with his home-town club, Swansea Town, in July 1964 and spent three years at Vetch Field before joining Northampton Town in November 1967. At the County Ground he made 62 league appearances before Arsenal paid £30,000 for his services in May 1969. During his first full season at Highbury, he played in 11 league games, followed in 1970–71 by winning a League Championship medal. He played in 18 league games during Arsenal's 'double' season. In addition he won the first of his 22 Welsh caps that campaign when he played against England. In October 1972, after having played in 81 league and cup games for the Gunners, he joined Birmingham City for a fee of £140,000. He went straight into the first team, making his début in a 1–0 home defeat by Manchester United, and in the club's next game, also at St Andrew's, he scored his only goal for the Blues in a 1–1 draw against Southampton. Over the next two seasons, Roberts was a regular in the heart of the Birmingham defence, usually alongside Roger Hynd, but after that he was constantly plagued by injuries and in four years with the club he only appeared in 79 games. In the summer of 1976, Roberts joined Wrexham for £30,000 and in 1977–78 he inspired the Robins to the Third Division Championship. He went on to play in 191 first-team games for Wrexham before moving to Hull City in 1980. He spent two seasons at Boothferry Park after which he retired through injury.

ROBINSON, ARTHUR Goalkeeper Arthur 'Nat' Robinson was one of the game's characters. No matter what the weather, Robinson always wore two jerseys, and when he was annoyed, he'd stand on his goal-line and whistle! Robinson was also one of the first keepers to develop the technique of running out of his penalty area to clear the ball with his feet. The Coventry-born keeper played his early football with Allesley, Coventry Stars and Singers FC before joining the Blues in the summer of 1898. He made his first-team début in a 3–2 home win over Walsall on the opening day of the 1898–99 season, going on to keep 11 clean sheets in a campaign in which he was ever present. In 1900-01, Robinson had a magnificent season, keeping 15 clean sheets and conceding just 24 goals as the Blues won promotion to the First Division. After just one season in the top flight the club were relegated, but in 1902–03 won promotion again, with Robinson once more in top form. He went on to appear in 306 league and cup games for the Blues before leaving in the summer of 1908 to join Chelsea. After two seasons at Stamford Bridge, he had a brief spell with Coventry before leaving the game.

ROBINSON, DAVE Centre-half Dave Robinson joined the Blues' ground-staff in the summer of 1964, signing professional forms two years later. After spending two seasons in the club's reserve side, he made his first-team début in September 1968, impressing in a 4–0 home win over Aston Villa. He kept his place in the City side for the remainder of the season, appearing in 29 games and scoring his first league goal for the club from the penalty-spot in a 3–1 home win over Blackburn Rovers. One of the club's most consistent players over the next two seasons, he was displaced by Stan Harland early in the club's Second Division promotion-winning season of 1971–72 and in March 1973 he left the club to join Walsall. Robinson, who had scored four goals in 127 games for the Blues, went on to serve the Saddlers for five years, appearing in 165 league games before hanging up his boots.

S

ST ANDREW'S St Andrew's was 'discovered' in 1906 by Harry Morris, a former player, director and chairman of the club. He asked a carpenter by the name of Harry Pumfrey to draw up the plans for the building and layout of the ground, while the clerk of the works was Tom Turley, who was prepared to work 14 hours a day 'without fee or reward, simply for sheer love of the old club'. It took Pumfrey and Turley's workforce almost ten months of hard labour to prepare St Andrew's at a total cost of £10,000. Yet it was estimated that these two enthusiasts had saved the club somewhere in the region of £2,000 in fees! Before a playing surface could be laid, the two large artesian springs which flooded the site had to be drained. After this, the holes were filled with brick, rubble and ash. Then, in order to raise terracing on the Coventry Road side, the site was offered as a tip and people paid the club to empty their rubbish there. It was estimated that thousands of tons were dumped there, earning the club £800. This banking was known as the Spion Kop, estimated to hold around 48,000 out of an overall capacity at the time of 75,000. Of those, 6,000 spectators could be seated in the Main Stand. The space under the seating housed the club's offices, dressing-room, a cycle store and a spacious billiard room for the players, paid for by local businessman and brewery owner, Sir John Holder. In fact, it was Holder who opened St Andrew's on Boxing Day 1906 after the club's directors had cleared snow from the pitch. A crowd of 32,000 saw the Blues play out a goalless draw against Middlesbrough in a game which kicked off an hour later than scheduled. The club promised to cover the terraces, especially at the Tilton Road End, which had been built into the side of a natural hill. Nevertheless, though roofs covered both the Kop and the Railway End when the ground recorded its record attendance of 67,341 against Everton in February 1929, the Tilton Road End was still uncovered. When the Second World War began, the Chief Constable closed St Andrew's for fear of air raids – it was the only ground in the country to be so affected. Though the ban was lifted some six months later, the ground was subsequently damaged by around twenty bombs. In 1942 the Main Stand burned down and the club played its wartime games at Leamington and Villa Park until 1943. After the hostilities had ended, the Kop was re-roofed and a new two-tier Main Stand built in the 1950s. In 1956 floodlights were erected and first switched on for a friendly against Borussia Dortmund. Following the club's entry into the Fairs Cup and the resulting successes, the Tilton Road End was finally covered. Over the ensuing years, however, the St Andrew's ground became rather drab and very basic. There were numerous ideas bandied about – a groundshare with Walsall; sharing a new stadium with Coventry City; a move to a new Olympic Stadium at the NEC; a new £35-million all-seater stadium – none of which came to fruition. In March 1993, City's new owner David Sullivan announced an impressive £4.5 million scheme to rebuild the Kop and Tilton Road End and, despite the club's relegation to the Second Division, work began in April 1994. The new Kop and Tilton Road stands were officially opened on 15 November 1994, when a crowd of 19,766 saw the Blues and Aston Villa draw 1–1 in a friendly. The St Andrew's ground now has an all-seater capacity of 25,812, whilst there are plans to continue the Tilton Road stand round to the Main Stand and then build a free-standing two-tier Railway Stand.

SAUNDERS, RON A bustling all-action centre-forward, Ron Saunders made his league début for Everton but, after only three league appearances, he moved to non-league Tonbridge. His league career was resurrected by Gillingham but Portsmouth saw his potential and he went on to score 156 goals in 258 games for Pompey before later playing for Watford and Charlton Athletic. Saunders started on the road to management with Yeovil Town in 1968 but joined Oxford United after 12 months. Obviously impressed with his work at the Manor Ground, Norwich City offered him their manager's post in 1969. After taking the Canaries to the Second Division Championship in 1971–72 and to the final of the League Cup, he resigned after a poor start to

Ron Saunders

the 1973–74 season. He had five months in charge of Manchester City before joining Aston Villa in the summer of 1974. Saunders transformed a disappointing Villa side into League Cup winners and runners-up in the Second Division in his first season in charge and was named Manager of the Year. In 1980–81 Villa won their first League Championship since 1910. They had reached the European Cup quarter-final the following season when Saunders resigned, surprisingly, to become manager of Birmingham City. After the club were relegated in 1983-84, he led them to promotion from the Second Division at the first attempt, but in January 1986, with the Blues again in trouble, he left to take charge of West Bromwich Albion. He failed to prevent the Baggies from being relegated and was sacked in September 1987.

SCHOFIELD, JOHNNY Goalkeeper Johnny Schofield began his career with Nuneaton Borough before being signed by the Blues in February 1950 as cover for England international Gil Merrick. He made his Birmingham début in a 3-0 defeat at Bury in October 1952 and, though he only made 11 league appearances over the next two seasons, he didn't let the club down when he had an extended run in the side at the end of the 1954-55 season. Playing in 11 of the last 12 games, he was only on the losing side once as the Blues won the Second Division Championship. It was 1959-60 before he won a regular place in the City side, missing just two of that season's games. In November 1960 he fractured his skull in Birmingham's 3-1 home win over Manchester United whilst diving at the feet of Alex Dawson, but thankfully he recovered to take his place in the side again early the following season. He was a member of the Birmingham Fairs Cup final teams of 1960 and 1961 and won a League Cup winners' tankard in 1963 after the Blues had beaten Aston Villa over two legs. He had appeared in 237 games for the club when in the summer of 1966 he joined Wrexham. After 62 appearances for the Robins, he moved into non-league football with Atherstone Town, Bromsgrove and Tamworth before managing Atherstone.

SEAMAN, DAVID England international goalkeeper David Seaman began his career with Leeds United after he had represented Rotherham Schoolboys. He became an apprentice at Elland Road in March 1980, turning professional in September 1981. Unable to break into the Yorkshire club's first team because of the consistency of John Lukic, he was transferred to Peterborough United for £4,000 in August 1982. His brilliant form for 'The Posh' was noted by Birmingham City manager Jim

David Seaman

Smith who paid £100,000 for his services in October 1984. He made his début for the Blues in a 2–0 defeat at Brighton but by the end of his first season at St Andrew's, he had helped the club to promotion to the First Division. However, in 1985–86, despite being ever present and winning England Under-21 honours, he could not save City from relegation and in order to remain in play in the top flight, he joined Queen's Park Rangers for £225,000 in August 1986. In four seasons at Loftus Road he was a first-team fixture and in 1988–89 he won the first of his 49 caps for England when appearing against Scotland. In May 1990, Arsenal paid out a record British fee for a goalkeeper of £1.3 million when obtaining Seaman's services. His impact on the Gunners' side in his first season was remarkable for not only did he help them win the League Championship, but he broke two club records when conceding only 18 league goals and keeping 24 clean sheets. Ever present again in 1991–92, he followed this in 1992–93 by helping the club to the FA and Coca Cola Cup double. In 1993–94 he helped the Gunners win the European Cup Winners' Cup and was a member of the Arsenal side which did the 'double' in 1997–98. Now in his tenth season with the Highbury club, he has currently made 377 first-team appearances for Arsenal.

SECOND DIVISION Birmingham have had 11 spells in the Second Division: after winning the inaugural season's Championship in 1892–93, the club had to play Test matches against Newton Heath for the right to play in the First Division. They lost, however, after a replay. They won promotion the following season but were back in the Second Division for the 1896–97 campaign after two seasons of top-flight football. The club's second spell lasted five seasons, during which time they were never out of the top eight before winning promotion as runners-up to Grimsby Town in 1900–01. Though they were relegated after one season, they made a quick return as runners-up to Manchester City in 1902–03. After five seasons in the First Division, the Blues returned to play nine seasons of Second Division football either side of the First World War before winning the Championship in 1920–21. The club won the Championship again in 1947–48 in what was their fifth spell in Division Two. A third Second Division title came their way again in 1954–55. After that, following ten seasons of First Division football, they returned to Division Two for the 1965–66 season. With the exception of 1969–70, the Blues were always in the top half of the table before winning promotion behind Norwich City in 1971–72. The club's eighth spell lasted just one season as they returned to the top flight in third place in 1979–80. Birmingham's next spell in the Second Division also lasted just one season as they won promotion in 1984–85 as runners-up to Oxford United. Their next spell lasted three seasons, however, before they were relegated to the Third Division for the first time in their history. The club's last spell in the Second Division following reorganisation saw them win the Championship in 1994–95.

SEMI-FINALS Up to the end of the 1998–99 season, the Blues had been involved in eight FA Cup semi-finals and two League Cup semi-finals as well as appearing at the same stage of the Inter Cities Fairs Cup, Leyland Daf and Auto Windscreen Shield competitions.

SIMMS, CHARLIE Charlie Simms served the Blues in a variety of capacities for over 30 years. He played for Mitchell St George's before joining Birmingham in the summer of 1884. A regular member of the club's first team for the next five years, he suffered a horrific knee injury which kept him out of the game for over two years. After overcoming that setback he made just one Football League appearance in a 4–3 win at Lincoln City during the club's Second Division Championship-winning season of 1892–93. After hanging up his boots, he became the club's trainer, a position he held for 10 years before becoming the club's groundsman. In January 1914, he was forced to give this job up due to ill-health.

SIMOD CUP The Simod Cup replaced the Full Members' Cup for the 1987–88 season. The Blues' first match saw them knocked out of the competition when they lost 3–1 at Derby County. In 1988–89 the club were well and truly beaten 6–0 by Aston Villa and so once again failed to progress past the first round.

SMALLEST PLAYER Although such statistics are always unreliable regarding those playing before the turn of the century, the distinction of being Birmingham's smallest player must go to Bobby Laing at 5ft 4ins. After playing for the Blues during the Second World War, he scored after five minutes of his league début and netted another in a 5–2 home win over Leeds United in February 1948.

SMITH, JIM A typically tough Yorkshireman, Jim Smith played

Jim Smith

with Sheffield United, Aldershot, Halifax Town and Lincoln City before becoming player–manager at non-league Boston United. His success here led to his being appointed manager of Colchester United in 1972, where he immediately rewarded their faith in him by winning promotion to the Third Division. When Jim Smith arrived at Blackburn Rovers in the summer of 1975, he inherited a winning team and a crowd with high expectations of success. After making sure Rovers retained their newly won Second Division status, Smith began to build a Blackburn side which reflected his approach to the game. However, although his team were capable of playing exciting, attacking football, they were also unpredictable, and as the promotion flame of the 1977–78 campaign began to die, Jim Smith accepted the managership of Birmingham City and within a matter of weeks had taken Norman Bodell, his assistant, with him. He enjoyed mixed fortunes at St Andrew's as the Blues were relegated in 1978–79 but won promotion 12 months later. After just two wins from the opening 14 games of the 1980–81 season, Smith was asked to leave. 'Bald Eagle', as he is affectionately known, had a few months out of the game before joining Oxford United. He took the unfashionable Manor Ground club from Third to First Division before moving to Loftus Road to manage Queen's Park Rangers. In 1988 he accepted the challenge to manage Newcastle United and in his time at St James Park restored some pride on Tyneside. He then took charge at Portsmouth where he led the club to an FA Cup semi-final and the play-offs before being appointed manager of Derby County in the summer of 1995. In his first season with the Rams, he led the club to promotion to the Premier Division where, after three seasons in the top flight, they are currently pushing for a place in Europe.

SMITH, TREVOR After playing in the same schools' side as Duncan Edwards, centre-half Trevor Smith joined the Blues as an amateur in the summer of 1951 and the following year was a member of the Birmingham side which won the European Youth Cup in Switzerland. He made his first-team début in a 4–2 win at Derby County in October 1953 and, though Army service was to disrupt his progress later in the decade, he was the club's first-choice pivot for 11 seasons. In 1954–55 he helped the Blues win the Second Division Championship and won international recognition for Engalnd at 'B' and Under-23 levels. In 1956 he was a member of the Birmingham side that lost 3–1 to Manchester City in the FA Cup final. His outstanding performances at the heart of the Blues' defence were eventually rewarded when he won two full caps for England in 1959. Replacing Billy Wright, he played against Wales at Ninian Park and Sweden at Wembley. A year later he played in the Inter Cities Fairs Cup final and in 1963 helped the Blues beat Aston Villa in the League Cup final. Trevor Smith went on to appear in 430 first-team games for the St Andrew's club before leaving in October 1964 to join Walsall for a fee of £18,000. After just 11 league games for the Saddlers, he decided to retire.

SPONSORS The club's present sponsors are Auto Windscreens. Previous sponsors have included Triton, Mark One, Evans Halshaw and P.J. Evans.

STEWART, JACKIE A former miner, winger Jackie Stewart began his football career with Raith Rovers and scored a good number of goals for the Scottish League club in his time at Stark's Park. He joined Birmingham in January 1948 and played his first game for the club in a 1–0 win at Luton Town. He played in the remaining 17 games of the season and scored vital goals in helping the club win the Second Division Championship. In 1948–49 he was the club's leading scorer with 11 goals in 37 league games including all four in the 4–1 home win over Manchester City on 15 September 1948. He continued to be a regular member of the Blues' first team until midway through the 1954–55 season but, following the arrival of Gordon Astall and Alex Govan, Stewart, who had scored 57 goals in 218 games, left St Andrew's and returned to Raith Rovers where he became the club's trainer.

STOKER, LEWIS Born at Wheatley Hill, County Durham, Lewis Stoker joined the Blues as a professional in September 1930 and made his first-team début in a 2–0 home win over Huddersfield Town on 6 December 1930. After establishing himself in the side in 1931–32, he was a virtual ever-present for the next five seasons, missing very few games. A great favourite with the fans, he enjoyed nothing more than driving forward from his position in midfield to support the attack, though he himself only scored two goals during his 246 first-team appearances for the club. The second of these proved to be the winner against Brentford in November 1935. After representing the Football League against the Irish League in 1932–33, he won three full caps for England, his first against Wales later that season. In May 1938 he left St

Andrew's to join Nottingham Forest but sadly, after just 12 league appearances for the City Ground club, the war ended his career prematurely.

STOKES, FRANK Burslem-born right-back Frank Stokes played for Burslem Park before joining Port Vale in October 1898. He became a regular in the Valiants side and had appeared in 82 matches when he joined Reading in the summer of 1901. After signing for the Blues he immediately formed a good full-back partnership with John Glover and, after his début against Blackburn Rovers in October 1903, he went on to make 199 appearances in seven seasons with the club. Stokes scored only one goal for the Blues, but what a goal it was – hit with ferocious power from almost 40 yards out, it made up a 2–0 home win over Notts County. Sadly, Stokes did not appear in his own benefit match, since he was chosen to play for the reserves on the afternoon of the game!

STORER, HARRY The son of a famous England and Liverpool goalkeeper and nephew of a Derbyshire and England cricketer, he had trials with Notts County and Millwall before turning professional with Grimsby Town. At Blundell Park he developed into a tough-tackling wing-half and in 1921 moved to Derby County for £4,500. During the 1923–24 season he played at inside-forward and after scoring 27 goals in 42 games was rewarded with the first of two full caps for England. In February 1929 he moved to Burnley for a large fee after scoring 63 goals in 274 games for the Rams. After two years at Turf Moor he became manager of Coventry City and steered the Sky Blues into the Second Division in 1935–36 until he made a surprise move from Highfield Road in 1945 to take charge of the Blues – probably on the premise that he had achieved all he could at Coventry. In his first season at St Andrew's, he led the Blues to the semi-finals of the FA Cup where they lost after a replay to his former club, Derby County, and to the Football League (South) Championship. In 1947–48 he took Birmingham to the Second Division Championship but by November 1948 he was back at Highfield Road. He remained with Coventry until December 1953 and after a spell out of management took over the reins at Derby County, where he succeeded in taking the Rams into the

Second Division. He stayed in charge until his retirement in 1962, later scouting for the club until his death five years later.

STURRIDGE, SIMON Brother of Derby County's Dean, the diminutive striker began his Football League career with Birmingham City and made his début as a substitute in a 4–1 home defeat by West Bromwich Albion in October 1988. He won a regular place in the Blues' line-up in 1989–90, playing in 31 league games and scoring 10 goals. The following season he helped the club win the Leyland Daf Cup and in 1991–92 scored 10 goals in the club's promotion-winning season. Injuries and a loss of form reduced his appearances in 1992–93 and at the end of that season, after which he had scored 38 goals in 186 games, he was transferred to Stoke City for £75,000. After an impressive first season at the Victoria Ground, he suffered a cruciate knee ligament injury. He had just returned to first-team action before damaging the cruciate in his other knee in a match at Rochdale. Thankfully the Potters have extended his contract for another term, for in his three seasons with the club he has only made 87 appearances and scored 15 goals.

SUBSTITUTES The first-ever Birmingham City substitute was Brian Sharples who came on for Ron Wylie against Preston North End at Deepdale on 28 August 1965. The club had to wait until 18 December 1965 for their first goalscoring substitute – Ronnie Fenton, scoring in the 4–0 home win over Bury. Geoff Vowden came on as a substitute against Huddersfield Town in September 1968 and scored a hat-trick in a 5–1 win. The greatest number of substitutes used in a single season by the Blues under the single substitute rule was 29 in seasons 1978–79 and 1985–86. From 1986–87, two substitutes were allowed and in 1994–95, the club used 77. For the last few seasons three substitutes have been allowed and in 1997–98, 113 were used. José Domínguez and Kevin Francis hold the club record for the most individual appearances as a substitute in one season, with 18 in seasons 1994–95 and 1997–98 respectively.

SUMMERILL, PHIL An England Youth international, he made his Football League début in a 2–1 home defeat by Carlisle United in March 1967. After making just four league appearances over the next two seasons, he claimed a regular first-team place in 1968–69 and ended the campaign as the club's leading scorer with 16 goals in 30 league games including hat-tricks against Hill City (Home 5–2) and Bolton Wanderers (Home 5–0). He scored in the opening three games of the 1969–70 season and netted a hat-trick in a 4–3 defeat at Carlisle United, ending the season as the Blues' top scorer with 13 goals. He was top scorer again in 1970–71 with a best-ever total of 21 goals in 46 games. After helping the club win promotion to the First Division in 1971–72, he found it difficult to hold down a first-team place and in January 1973, after scoring 52 goals in 131 games, he left to join Huddersfield Town. He scored 11 goals in 54 league games for the Terriers before signing for Millwall where he netted 20 goals in 87 games. He later ended his league career with Wimbledon before playing non-league football for Highgate United, Atherstone Town and Redditch United.

SUSTAINED SCORING During the 1898–99 season, Walter Abbott scored 34 goals in 34 games to set a league scoring record for the Blues. He scored two on the opening day of the season in a 6–2 win at Burton Swifts and six in the first four games of the campaign. He netted five goals in an 8–0 home win over Darwen and hat-tricks against Loughborough Town (Home 6–0), Woolwich Arsenal (Home 4–1), Luton Town (Away 3–2) and Gainsborough Trinity (Home 6–1).

T

TAIT, PAUL Combative midfielder Paul Tait was a product of the club's youth set-up and made his first-team début as a substitute in the final game of the 1987–88 season in a goalless home draw against Leeds United. Though he was always an important member of the Blues' squad, injuries reduced his number of first-team appearances. However, in 1994–95 he helped the club win the Second Division Championship and beat Carlisle United 1–0 in the final of the Auto Windscreen Shield. In fact it was Paul Tait, who had come on as a substitute, who scored the only goal of the final in 'sudden death' after the game had finished goalless after extra time. At one stage during the 1995–96 season it looked as if he would be joining Coventry City, but the move fell through and he fought his way back into first-team contention. After losing his place just after Christmas 1996, he asked to get on the transfer list. Eventually he agreed to a new contract, which included a testimonial on his reaching ten years at St Andrew's. The club's longest-serving player, he had a loan spell with Northampton Town before returning to St Andrew's for 1998–99, his testimonial year.

TALLEST PLAYER The tallest player on Birmingham City's books has been Kevin Francis at 6ft 7ins. Sadly, the former Stockport County player who joined the Blues for £800,000 suffered a series of injuries during his time at St Andrew's.

TARANTINI, ALBERTO Argentinian international Alberto Tarantini, who played for his country against Holland in the 1978 World Cup final, joined the Blues from Boca Juniors in October of that year. He made his Football League début in a 1–0 defeat at Tottenham Hotspur, lining up against his Argentinian team-mate Ossie Ardiles. A week later, the talented Argentinian made his home début in the local derby against Aston Villa in a match watched by a crowd of 36,145, more than double the season's average! Though he was a world-class player and had won 59 caps for his country, Tarantini couldn't take to the English game and in April 1979 his contract was cancelled. In a season in which the Blues lost their First Division status, Tarantini appeared in 24 games, his only goal coming in a 1–1 home draw against Bristol City. He went back to Argentina and played for both Talleres Córdoba and River Plate before returning to play in Europe with French clubs Bastia and Toulouse and later Urania Geneva in Switzerland.

TAYLOR, GORDON Now secretary of the Professional Footballers' Association, Gordon Taylor once scored 97 goals in a season as a schoolboy. He played at inside-forward and captained Ashton Boys to the sixth round of the English Schools' Trophy, also appearing three times for Lancashire Boys. Having supported Bolton as a boy, he jumped at the chance of joining the Bolton Wanderers when they asked him to sign amateur forms. He made his league début in March 1963 at Wolverhampton Wanderers and in 1964–65 was ever present as the Lancashire club just missed out on a quick return to Division One following their relegation the previous season. He went on to score 46 goals in 286 league and cup games for Bolton until he was transferred to Birmingham City for £18,000 in December 1970. At St Andrew's, Taylor helped the club win promotion to the First Division in 1971–72 and reach the FA Cup semi-finals that season and in 1974–75. His accurate crosses from the flanks provided Bob Hatton, Kenny Burns, Bob Latchford and Trevor Francis with a great number of chances. Taylor had scored 10 goals in 203 first-team outings for the Blues when in March 1976 he moved to Blackburn Rovers. After two years at Ewood Park and a season with Vancouver Whitecaps, he joined Bury where he ended his league career.

TEST MATCHES In 1892, the Football League decided there would be no admission to the First Division without having competed in the Second. Promotion to the First Division would not be automatic, either. Instead, there were to be Test matches. The top three in the Second Division would play against the bottom three from the First Division in sudden-death play-offs. The Blues finished worthy winners of the Second Division in the inaugural season and completed the campaign with a run of nine straight wins. Their opponents, Newton Heath, finished bottom of the First Division. The match was played at the Victoria Ground, Stoke, where after 20 minutes Farman netted for Newton Heath, albeit against the run of play. In the second half, Wheldon hit a post before scoring the equaliser with another tremendous shot. Although both sides had further chances, the game finished with honours even. The replay at Olive Grove, Sheffield, the following Thursday saw Mobley put the Blues ahead in the sixth minute before Wheldon hit a post. Newton Heath equalised from the penalty spot following a foul by Bayley. In the second half Newton Heath took the lead but, within seconds, Walton had equalised for the Blues. They continued to create chances but it was Newton Heath who ran out winners 5–2 to keep their First Division status. Receipt of the new Second Division Championship Shield was a small consolation for the Birmingham club. The following season the Blues again featured in the Test matches. They did not make the same mistake again and were promoted to the First Division after beating Darwen 3–1 with goals from Hallam, Walton and Wheldon. The club's last involvement in the Test matches was at the end of the 1895–96 season. The Blues, who had finished fifteenth in the First Division, had to play both Liverpool and Manchester City who were the top two clubs in the Second Division. The Blues lost 4–0 at Anfield and could only draw 0–0 at home to Liverpool. After suffering a 3–0 defeat against Manchester City at Hyde Road, the Blues won the return 8–0 with both Jones and Wheldon scoring hat-tricks, but it wasn't enough: after two seasons in Division One, the club were relegated.

TEXACO CUP The predecessor of the Anglo–Scottish Cup, it was launched in 1970–71 and was for those English, Irish and Scottish club sides not involved in European competitions. The Blues first entered in 1973–74 and after both legs of their first-round tie against Stoke City had ended goalless, they won 3–1 on penalties. In round two, City drew 1–1 at home to Newcastle United which was also the scoreline in the second leg when after 10 minutes of extra-time the game was abandoned because of bad light. In the rearranged fixture, the Magpies won 3–1 to take the tie on aggregate 4–2. In 1974–75, the Blues drew their first two group matches against West Bromwich Albion (Away 0–0) and Peterborough United (Away 0–0) before beating Norwich City (Home 3–1). In the second round, Ayr United were beaten 3–0 at St Andrew's after which the sides played out a goalless draw at Somerset Park to take City into the semi-finals where they met last seasons winners, Newcastle United. After a Bob Hatton goal had given Birmingham a 1–1 draw at St James Park, a crowd of 17,754 turned up at St Andrew's for the second leg, but the Blues were well and truly beaten on the night, 4–1, by a Newcastle side that went on to retain the trophy.

THIRD DIVISION The Blues have had just one spell in the Third Division following their relegation in 1988–89. After finishing seventh in 1989–90 and twelfth the following season, City won promotion in 1991–92 when they finished runners-up to Brentford. They won their first four matches of the season and were undefeated in the opening seven, which ended their campaign with 81 points, just one behind the Bees.

THOMAS, MARTIN Goalkeeper Martin Thomas began his Football League career with Bristol Rovers. The Welsh Youth and Under-21 international made 162 league appearances for the then Eastville club, but towards the end of his career with the Pirates he was loaned out to Cardiff City and Southend United before Newcastle United paid £50,000 for his services in March 1983. His arrival at St James Park started a healthy rivalry with Kevin Carr. Thomas eventually won the senior's place, though, and in 1986–87 represented Wales at full international level against Finland. He had appeared in 131 games for the Magpies when he moved to Birmingham City in October 1988. He made his début in a 1–0 home defeat by Plymouth Argyle and, though he turned in a number of memorable performances over the rest of the season, the Blues were relegated to the Third Division. His penalty saves against Swansea City in 1991 were a major factor in the club's Leyland Daf Cup success. He went on to appear in 157 games for the Blues before leaving the club at the end of the 1991–92 season.

THOMSON, ROBERT A. Bobby Thomson began his Football League career with Wolverhampton Wanderers and, after serving a two-year apprenticeship, made his first-team début in a 2–1 FA Cup fourth-round defeat at home to West Bromwich Albion. A polished performer, he soon established himself as a first-team regular and developed into an international player, winning eight full caps for England before the age of 22. He also played for the Under-23s and Football League and, in 1966–67, helped the Molineux club win promotion to the First Division. He had played in 300 games for Wolves when Birmingham City paid £40,000 for his services in March 1969. He made his début for the Blues in a goalless draw at Portsmouth and appeared in the last ten games of the season. He was ever present in 1969–70 as City finished eighteenth in the Second Division, but then lost his place to Ray Martin. With Gary Pendrey also coming through, Thomson, who had made 69 appearances, left to join Luton Town, having had a short loan spell with Walsall while at St Andrew's. He later ended his league career with Port Vale before dropping into non-league football as player–manager of Stafford Rangers.

THOMSON, ROBERT G. After playing as an amateur with Albion Rovers and Airdrieonians, Bobby Thomson joined Wolverhampton Wanderers in 1953. However, competition at Molineux in those days was very tough and in five years he made only one league appearance. In June 1959 he joined Aston Villa and scored on his début in a 3–0 home win over Sunderland. Partnering Jimmy MacEwan on the right, the aggressive Scot scored 20 goals in 34 league games as Villa won the Second Division Championship. The following season he won a League Cup winners' medal as Villa beat Rotherham United and in 1962–63 he played in another League Cup final, scoring Villa's goal in a 3–1 defeat by Birmingham City over two legs. He had scored 70 goals in 171 games before joining the Blues in September 1963. His first game for the St Andrew's club saw him score City's goal in a 2–1 defeat at Sheffield Wednesday and though he was never as prolific a scorer as in his Villa days, he gave the Blues equally good service. He was an important member of the Birmingham side for over four seasons but in December 1967, after scoring 25 goals in 129 games, he left to end his league career with Stockport County.

TODD, COLIN Colin Todd was an elegant and poised player who was always comfortable on the ball. He began his career with Sunderland and had made 173 league appearances for the Wearsiders when he joined Derby County for £170,000 in February 1971. He developed a great partnership with Roy McFarland and won two League Championship medals at the Baseball Ground under Brian Clough and later Dave Mackay. In the latter of those championship-winning seasons, 1974–75, Todd rarely made an error and was voted the PFA's Footballer of the Year. After playing in 371 games for the Rams he moved to Everton for £300,000 in September 1978. Within 12 months he had joined Birmingham City and made his début as a substitute in a 2–2 draw at Orient. At the end of his first season he helped the Blues win promotion to the First Division but after three years at St Andrew's, in which he appeared in 108 games, he signed for Nottingham Forest for a fee of £70,000. He later played for Oxford United, where he helped them win the Third Division title in 1983–84, Luton Town and Vancouver Whitecaps before retiring in 1985. After managing Whitley Bay he was assistant-manager to Bruce Rioch at Middlesbrough, eventually succeeding him as manager. He resigned, surprisingly, in 1991 and a year later became assistant-manager to Rioch again, this time at Bolton Wanderers. He played an important role in the club's promotion to the Premier League and when Rioch left to manage Arsenal, he remained as assistant to Roy McFarland before becoming manager when his former Derby colleague was dismissed. Since then, Todd has seen his side win the First Division Championship and suffer relegation from the Premiership and participate in the play-offs.

TRANSFERS The club's record transfer fee received is £2.5 million from Coventry City for Gary Breen in January 1997. The club's record transfer fee paid is £1.85 million to Port Vale for Jon McCarthy in September 1997.

TREMELLING, DAN Goalkeeper Dan Tremelling, who was affectionately known as the 'India-rubber man', played his early football with Shirebrook Juniors before joining Lincoln City at the end of the First World War. His outstanding performances for the Imps prompted Birmingham to sign him and he made his

Colin Todd

début in a 4–1 home win over Hull City on the opening day of the 1919–20 season. Tremelling was the club's only ever-present during a campaign in which he kept 17 clean sheets. The following season he won a Second Division Championship medal. An ever-present in seasons 1923–24 and 1924–25, Tremelling missed very few games in 12 seasons with the Blues and was responsible for Cardiff City not winning the League title in

1923–24 – he saved Len Davies' last-minute penalty-kick which, had he scored, would have given the Bluebirds the League Championship. Tremelling won just one England cap while playing in a 2–1 defeat by Wales at Burnley in 1927, though he also represented the Football League. He played in 395 league and cup games for the Blues before losing his place to Harry Hibbs. After a spell with Bury, he returned to St Andrew's to become the club's trainer, a position he held for three years until the outbreak of the Second World War.

TRIGG, CYRIL Cyril Trigg joined Birmingham from Bedworth Town in the summer of 1935 and made his début at full-back in a 2–1 defeat at Aston Villa in a game watched by 50,000. After that, he missed very few games up until the outbreak of the Second World War, and scored his first goal for the club in a 2–1 home win over Middlesbrough on Boxing Day 1938. During the war, Trigg moved to centre-forward and scored 88 goals in 95 appearances, including five in a 6–2 home win over Stoke and 12 in four games in 1940–41. He also scored four against Walsall in 1943–44 and against Port Vale in 1944–45. Trigg also 'guested' for Blackpool and Nottingham Forest, and in 1945–46 he played most of his games at right-back, helping the club win the League (South) title. In 1946–47 he was the club's top scorer with 19 league and cup goals in 33 games including a hat-trick in a 3–1 win at Luton Town. He reverted to right-back for the first half of the following season before seeing out the campaign in which the Blues won the Second Division Championship at centre-forward. He top scored for the club again in 1950–51, his total of 19 goals in 36 games including his second league hat-trick in a 5–0 home win over Swansea Town. He went on to score 72 goals in 291 league and cup games before leaving St Andrew's to become player–coach at Stourbridge.

TURNER, ARTHUR Arthur Turner served Birmingham City for 13 years as a player, then as a manager. He played his football at Wolstanton PSA and Downings Tileries and worked as an upholsterer when he signed amateur forms for West Bromwich Albion. He never got a game at the Hawthorns when he lost his job and applied for a job at Stoke. There, he signed as an amateur in November 1930 but was very quickly moved to full-time forms.

At Stoke he captained the side for a number of seasons and played in 118 consecutive league games for the club between 1935 and 1938. After scoring 17 goals in 312 games he signed for the Blues but found that, within six months of him joining the St Andrew's club, war had been declared. During the hostilities, he appeared in 172 wartime games and skippered the side which won the League (South) Championship and reached the FA Cup semi-finals in 1946. After appearing in 53 league and cup games for Birmingham, he joined Southport before retiring in 1949 to become Crewe's manager. In 1950 he moved to become assistant-manager to Bob McGrory at Stoke before taking over at St Andrew's. Within six months of his appointment, he led the Blues to the Second Division Championship and the following season took them to a Wembley Cup final. He left St Andrew's in 1958 to become manager of Oxford United the following year. He led them into the Football League in 1962, promotion in 1965 and then to the Third Division Championship in 1968. After leaving the Manor Ground he scouted for Rotherham United for a few years.

U

UNDEFEATED Birmingham City have remained undefeated at home throughout seasons: 1892–93, 1902–03 and 1971–72. The club's best and longest undefeated home sequence in the Football League is 36 matches, between 20 October 1970 and 25 April 1972. City's longest run of undefeated league matches home and away is 20, between 3 September 1994 and 2 January 1995.

UNUSUAL GOALS One of the most unusual goals was scored against Wolves on 13 November 1920. Percy Barton, the Blues' wing-half who later played at full-back, headed home the third goal in a 4–1 win from fully 30 yards! Another unusual goal occurred when goalkeeper Martin Thomas stepped over his own goal-line with the ball in his hands for the winning goal in a 2–1 defeat against Shrewsbury Town at St Andrew's in March 1989.

UTILITY PLAYERS A utility player is one of those particularly gifted footballers who can play in several, or even many, different positions. Tom Fillingham (1929–1938) played in seven different positions for the Blues and Jack Badham (1946–1959) played in eight different positions. Dennis Jennings (1935–1950) played in every position except centre-half during his Birmingham career. After the mid-1960s, players were encouraged to become more adaptable. At the same time, however, much less attention came to be paid to the implication of wearing a certain numbered shirt and, accordingly, some of the more versatile players came to wear almost all the different numbered shirts at some stage or another, although this did not necessarily indicate a vast variety of positions. In the modern game, Jimmy Calderwood and Brian Roberts were talented enough to wear a variety of outfield shirts, while long-serving Malcolm Page played in every position except goalkeeper.

V

VAN DEN HAUWE, PAT An uncompromising, hard-tackling defender, Pat Van Den Hauwe was born in Dendermonde in Belgium and moved to live in London with his parents at a very early age. He joined Birmingham as an apprentice in the summer of 1976 and turned professional two years later. He made his début for the Blues in a 2–1 home defeat by Manchester City in October 1978 but had to wait until 1981–82 before winning a regular place in the City line-up. His progress was not helped by being called upon to alternate between full-back and central defence in a St Andrew's side continually struggling against the drop. Eventually settling at full-back, he was ever present in 1983–84 when the Blues were relegated. He was too good a player for Second Division football and left St Andrew's after 143 first-team appearances and joined Everton for £100,000. By the end of his first season at Goodison he had helped Everton win the League Championship, the European Cup Winners' Cup and reach the FA Cup final. During that season he also won the first of 13 Welsh international caps when he played against Spain. Over the next four years he was a regular in the Everton side which won the league title again in 1987 and reached the FA Cup finals in 1986 and 1989. He had played in 190 league and cup games for the Toffees by August 1989 when he moved to Tottenham Hotspur for a fee of £575,000. He finally collected an FA Cup winners' medal in May 1991 when Spurs beat Nottingham Forest and went on to play in 140 first-team games for the White Hart Lane club before ending his career with Millwall.

VICTORIES IN A SEASON – HIGHEST The highest number of wins in a season by the St Andrew's club is 25. They first achieved that number of victories in 1946–47 when they finished

Pat Van Den Hauwe

third in Division Two and then repeated the feat in 1984–85 when they ended the season as runners-up, again in Division Two. The club last won 25 league games in 1994–95 when they won the Second Division Championship, finishing four points ahead of Brentford.

VICTORIES IN A SEASON – LOWEST City's poorest performance was in 1978–79 when they won only six matches out of their 42 league games and finished twenty-first in the First Division.

VINCENT, JOHNNY Inside-forward Johnny Vincent joined the Blues straight from school and appeared in the club's Football Combination side when only 16 years old. After turning professional on his seventeenth birthday, he made his first-team début for the Blues in a 2–2 home draw against Blackburn Rovers in March 1964. However, it was 1966–67 before he won a regular place in the Birmingham side having developed into an attacking left-sided midfielder. Though he created many goalscoring opportunities for his team-mates, he possessed a powerful shot in his left foot and in 1967–68, when the Blues finished fourth in Division Two, Vincent had his best goal-scoring season: he found the net on 14 occasions, including in each of the opening three games of the season. He continued to play for the Blues until March 1971 when he left to join Middlesbrough for a fee of £40,000 after he had scored 44 goals in 194 games. Unable to settle at Ayresome Park, he moved to Cardiff City where he scored 11 goals in 66 league games including one against the Teesside club on his début for the Bluebirds. He left Ninian Park in the summer of 1975 and played non-league football for Atherstone Town before hanging up his boots.

VOWDEN, GEOFF Barnsley-born forward Geoff Vowden moved to Jersey with his family when he was only four, and was one of a number of players from the Channel Islands who began his career with Nottingham Forest. He spent four years at the City Ground, scoring 40 goals in 90 league games before moving to Birmingham City for a fee of £25,000 in October 1964. He scored on his début in a 3–0 home win over Blackpool and ended the campaign with 10 goals in 28 games. He was the Blues' leading scorer in 1965–66 and 1966–67 with 23 and 21 goals respectively. Included in his 1965–66 tally was his first hat-trick for the club in a 4–3 win at Rotherham United. Vowden's next hat-trick for the club was against Huddersfield Town in September 1968 when he came on as a substitute for Ron Wylie and helped City to a 5–1 win. He went on to score 94 goals in 253 league and cup games before joining Aston Villa for £12,000 in March 1971. In his first full season at Villa Park, he helped the club win the Third Division Championship but left league football after netting 25 goals in 113 outings, to become player–manager of Kettering Town. He later coached in Saudi Arabia before returning to live in the Nottingham area where he concentrated on coaching young players at local youth clubs and sports centres.

W

WALTON, BILLY Inside-forward Billy Walton joined the Blues as a 17-year-old and played for the club in the Alliance League for three years before making his Football League début at Sheffield United in September 1892. That season, Walton went on to score 14 goals in 19 games including a hat-trick in the 12–0 win over Walsall Town Swifts as Birmingham won the Second Division Championship. In 1893–94, when the club did win promotion to the top flight, Walton scored 16 goals in 20 games, and this after he had missed the opening six games of the season. His total included another hat-trick in a 5–2 home win over Grimsby Town. Walton gave the club great service and once agreed along with a number of his colleagues, to play for a month without pay to help the club out of the financial difficulties they were in. He had scored 63 goals in 200 league and cup games for the Blues when he left the club in 1903.

WANT, TONY A competent yet unspectacular full-back, Tony Want began his league career with Tottenham Hotspur but was perhaps unlucky to be at White Hart Lane at the same time as players like Cyril Knowles, Phil Beal and Joe Kinnear. An England Youth international, he had few opportunities with the London club and in the summer of 1972, after playing in 76 first-team games, he was allowed to move to Birmingham City for £50,000. After appearing in four Anglo–Italian Cup games, he made his league début for the Blues in a 2–1 home defeat at the hands of Sheffield United on the opening day of the 1972–73 season. He spent six years at St Andrew's, often turning out as a central defender. His only league goal in 101 games for the club came in November 1972 as Norwich City were beaten 4–1. In February 1978, Want's contract with the club was cancelled by mutual consent and, like many other players of his generation, he

Tony Want

finished his career in America, playing for Minnesota Kicks for four years.

WARHURST, ROY After playing as an amateur for Huddersfield Town during the early part of the Second World War, Roy

Warhurst signed professional forms for his home-town team, Sheffield United. He made 17 league appearances for the Blades before joining Birmingham for a fee of £8,000 in March 1950. He made his début for the Blues in a 1–0 home win over Manchester City and though the opposition didn't score in any of his three appearances at the end of that season, the club were relegated to the Second Division. After playing in just nine games in 1950–51, Warhurst became an established member of the Birmingham side and over the next six seasons scored 10 goals in 239 league and cup games. One of the best wing-halves in the country, he helped the Blues win the Second Division Championship in 1954–55 and reach the FA Cup final the following season, though he missed the Wembley game through injury. He also played in the club's FA Cup semi-final against Manchester United at Hillsborough before leaving at the end of that season to join Manchester City. He made 40 appearances for the Maine Road club before ending his league career with Crewe Alexandra and Oldham Athletic, having made 329 league appearances for his five clubs.

WARTIME FOOTBALL In spite of the outbreak of war in 1914, the major football leagues embarked upon their planned programme of matches for the ensuing season and these were completed on schedule at the end of April the following year. The season saw the club finish sixth in Division Two. The Blues did not play competitive football in 1915–16 but in the remaining years of the war, they played in the Midland Section's Principal and Subsidiary Tournaments. The club's best season was 1918–19 when they won the Subsidiary Tournament and finished runners-up to Nottingham Forest in the Principal Tournament. In contrast to the events of 1914, once war was declared on 3 September 1939, the Football League programme of 1939–40 was immediately suspended and the government forbade any major sporting events, so that for a while there was no football of any description. In 1939–40 the Blues finished third in the Football League Midland Section and in 1940–41 competed in the Football League (South) but only played 16 games due to the bomb damage at St Andrew's. After a season of playing friendlies, the club played in the Football League (North) in 1942–43 with their home games at Villa Park. After returning to St Andrew's, the club had two mediocre seasons in the regional competition before winning the Football League (South) Championship and reaching the FA Cup semi-finals in 1945–46.

WATTS, JOHNNY Able to play in any of the half-back line positions, Johnny Watts joined Birmingham City in the summer of 1951 after leaving the army. He made just one league appearance in the 1951–52 season when the Blues lost 4–0 at Swansea, but worse than the heavy defeat was the injury he received that kept him out of the game for three months. He was in and out of the Birmingham side during his first five seasons at St Andrew's but finally established himself during the 1956–57 season. After playing in the 1960 Fairs Cup final against Barcelona, Watts lost his place to Welsh international Terry Hennessey and asked for a transfer on a number of occasions. He was refused a move until 1963 when, after appearing in 248 league and cup games, he was allowed to leave and join Nuneaton Borough. He later ended his career playing under former City goalkeeper Gil Merrick at Bromsgrove Rovers.

WEALANDS, JEFF Darlington-born goalkeeper Jeff Wealands began his career with Wolverhampton Wanderers and turned professional with the Molineux club in October 1968. He never made their Football League side, however, and after a short spell on loan at Northampton Town he was transferred to his hometown team Darlington who had offered him terms in 1966. After appearing in 31 games for the Quakers he joined Hull City and in seven and a half years at Boothferry Park, he played in 270 league and cup games before joining the Blues for a fee of £30,000 in the summer of 1979. He made his début in a 2–0 defeat at Sunderland in the second game of the 1979–80 season but held his place to appear in 40 league games, keeping 16 clean sheets as the Blues won promotion to the First Division. Wealands was the club's first-choice keeper for the next two and a half seasons but, after playing in 117 games and having had a loan spell at Oldham Athletic, he joined Manchester United as cover for Gary Bailey. He made eight appearances for United before being allowed to join Altrincham following a troublesome back injury.

WHARTON, SID Outside-left Sid Wharton played his early football with Smethwick Wesleyan Rovers before joining

Jeff Wealands

Birmingham in November 1897. Within 24 hours of putting pen to paper, he had made his début for the Blues in a 4–0 defeat at Newcastle United. After appearing in only seven games that season, he established himself as a first-team regular at the beginning of the 1898–99 campaign and missed very few games over the next five seasons. Though not a prolific scorer, preferring instead to lay on chances for his team-mates with his low, accurate crosses, Wharton did score nine goals in 1899–1900. The following season he helped the Blues win promotion and did the same again in 1902–03. Wharton, who had represented the Football League and played for England against Germany in an unofficial international in 1902, was forced to give up the game in the summer of 1903 through injury. He stayed on at St Andrew's to coach before becoming a turf accountant in later years and an important name in the world of boxing as a master of ceremonies.

WHELDON, FREDDIE Known as 'Diamond', Freddie Wheldon was a superb dribbler of the ball who was capable of beating players before laying on chances for his team-mates or scoring himself. He joined the Blues as a professional in February 1890 after playing his early football with Rood End White Star and Langley Green Victoria. He made his first-team début later that month, scoring twice in a 6–2 Football Alliance win over Darwen. He was ever present in 1891–92, scoring 11 goals in 22 games including a hat-trick in a 7–1 home win over Bootle. During the club's first season in the Football League when they won the Second Division Championship, Wheldon was the Blues' top scorer with 25 goals in 22 games including hat-tricks in successive games as Lincoln City were beaten 4–3 at Sincil Bank and Northwich Victoria 6–2 at Muntz Street. Sadly the Blues were not promoted since they lost to Newton Heath in the Test matches. In 1893–94 the club were promoted as runners-up to Liverpool and Wheldon, who scored 22 goals in 28 appearances, netted four in an 8–0 home win over Northwich Victoria. In June 1896, after having scored 82 goals in 129 games, he was transferred to Aston Villa for £100 plus a further £250 from the proceeds of a specially arranged match. Though he scored 22 goals in 37 league and cup appearances in his first season at Villa Park, he had an even better season in 1897–98. He scored hat-tricks in each of the first two matches that season and ended the campaign as the club's leading goalscorer with 23 goals in 28 games. He was outstanding in season's 1898–99 and 1899–1900 as Villa made it three League Championship wins in four attempts. Wheldon won four caps for England, scoring a hat-trick on his début against Ireland in 1897. Against Scotland in 1898 he won a bicycle for scoring the first goal. After netting 74 goals in 138 first-team appearances, Wheldon was transferred to West Bromwich Albion but could not prevent their relegation to the Second Division. He later played for Queen's Park Rangers, Portsmouth and Worcester City before ending his career with Coventry City. An excellent county cricketer, Wheldon scored 4,869 runs for Worcestershire and helped dismiss 93 batsmen as a wicket-keeper.

WHITE, FRANK Outside-left Frank White was recommended to Birmingham by the club's international goalkeeper, Harry Hibbs. Though he was initially tried at centre-half, it was when he played on the wing that his career took off. He made his début for the St Andrew's club in a 1–0 defeat at Liverpool in April 1933 before establishing himself as a first-team regular the following season. Possessing great speed and a telling shot, his best season in terms of goals scored was 1934–35 when he netted 16 goals in 36 league and cup outings, including a hat-trick in a 3–0 home win over Preston North End. White actually joined the Deepdale club in December 1938 after scoring 50 goals in 156 games for the Blues. At North End he scored 10 goals in 19 outings in the last peacetime league season before 'guesting' for Aldershot, Mansfield, Sheffield United and Wrexham during the hostilities. He returned to St Andrew's for the 1945–46 season and played in a number of regional matches before entering non-league football with Redditch.

WHITTON, STEVE Steve Whitton began his career as a midfielder with Coventry City but under Dave Sexton's management, he was converted into a striker. A strongly built man, he made his league début for the Sky Blues in a 1–1 home draw against Spurs in September 1979 and in four years as Highfield Road, he scored 23 goals in 82 games including a hat-trick in a 3–1 win at Manchester City. On leaving the Sky Blues, he joined West Ham United but had a disappointing time at Upton Park, so in January 1986 he moved to the Blues on loan before signing on a permanent basis for a fee of £75,000 in the summer of that year. He made his début in a 1–0 win at Oxford United and held his place in the City side for three seasons but in March 1989, with the club struggling near the foot of the Second Division, Whitton, who had scored 35 goals in 119 games, joined Sheffield Wednesday for £275,000. After just under two years at Hillsborough he moved to Ipswich Town where he scored 19 goals in 105 league and cup games. In March 1994 he moved to Colchester United where he became the club's assistant-manager. A great favourite with the Layer Road crowd, he suffered cruciate and medial ligament damage in his second season with the club but recovered to play until the spring of 1998. At that point, a niggling neck injury forced him to retire after scoring 117 goals in 530 games for his six league clubs.

WIGLEY, STEVE Right-winger Steve Wigley was playing non-league football for Curzon Athletic when Brian Clough signed him for Nottingham Forest in March 1981. He went on to play in 82 league games for the City Ground club before joining Sheffield United. After making 32 league appearances for the Blades, Wigley arrived at St Andrew's in March 1987 in a player-exchange deal involving Martin Kuhl. Wigley made his début for the Blues in a 1–0 home defeat by Portsmouth and then scored the club's equalising goal in a 2–2 draw at Barnsley in his next game. The following season he missed just one game and went on to score five goals in 98 games before leaving to join Portsmouth for a fee of £350,000 in March 1989. A great favourite with the Pompey fans, he appeared in over 100 league games for the Fratton Park club before hanging up his boots.

WIGMORE, WALTER After playing his early football with Kiveton Park, Worksop and Sheffield United, Walter Wigmore joined Gainsborough Trinity where he scored 22 goals in 52 league games before signing for the Blues. When he arrived at the club he was a centre-forward but, midway through the 1899–1900 season, he was converted to centre-half with great effect. In fact, his performances won him representative honours with the Football League. Wigmore spent 12 seasons with Birmingham, helping the club win promotion in 1900–01 and again in 1902–03. He went on to score 25 goals in 355 league and cup games for the Blues, his last appearance coming in February 1912 when a Jack Hall hat-trick helped Birmingham beat Wolverhampton Wanderers 3–1. After leaving the Blues, Wigmore had one season playing non-league football for Brierley Hill before leaving the game.

WILCOX, FREDDIE Freddie Wilcox played his early football with Bristol Rovers in the Southern League, scoring 19 goals in

61 games before joining the Blues for a fee of £150 in March 1903. He scored twice on his début as Blackpool were beaten 5–1. Then, in only his fourth game for the club, he scored four goals as the Blues demolished Doncaster Rovers 12–0. He ended the season scoring seven goals in his six appearances as Birmingham won promotion to the First Division. His best goal-scoring season for the Blues was 1904–05 when he netted 12 goals in 28 games including a hat-trick in a 4–1 home win over Wolves. His form that season led to his winning a trial for England but in March 1906 after scoring 32 goals in 84 games, he left to join Middlesbrough. There he formed a prolific goalscoring partnership with Steve Bloomer and in 1908–09 the pair of them scored 51 goals with Wilcox claiming 20. After switching to centre-half, he was forced to retire from the game after damaging his knee whilst playing for 'Boro.

WITHERS, COLIN An England Schoolboy international goalkeeper, Colin Withers was on amateur forms with West Bromwich Albion when the Blues offered him professional terms in May 1957. He made his first-team début for the club in a goalless draw at home to Plymouth Argyle in a League Cup tie before making his first appearance in the league side three days later. Sadly, Withers had a nightmare of a game as City went down 6–0 to Tottenham Hotspur at White Hart Lane. He put that performance behind him, however, and went on to play in 116 first-team games for the Blues before signing for Aston Villa for £18,000 in November 1964. Remarkably, Withers's league début for Villa was also at Tottenham but this time he only conceded four goals as the Villans went down 4–0. In 1965–66 he played in all but four games which were lost and in 1966–67 he was ever present. In these two seasons, he was the supporters' Player of the Year. He appeared in 163 league and cup games for Villa before being transferred to Lincoln City in the summer of 1969. He made only one appearnce for the Sincil Bank club before going to Holland to play for Go Ahead Deventer. He later returned to England to play out his career with Atherstone Town.

WITHOUT REPLY During October and November 1898, Birmingham scored 35 goals without reply in four League and FA Cup games. They beat Chirk 8–0 in the FA Cup, Luton Town 9–0 in the League and then Druids 10–0 in the Cup before beating Darwen 8–0 in the League. Goalkeeper Jack Clutterbuck hardly touched the ball in six hours play!

WOMACK, FRANK The holder of the club's Football League appearance record and one of the Blue's greatest players, Frank Womack gave 20 years' loyal service to the St Andrew's club after joining them from Rawmarsh FC in the summer of 1908. He made his début in a 3–1 away win at Gainsborough Trinity on 5 September 1908 and went on to appear in 491 league games, playing the last on 10 April 1928 when the Blues were beaten 2–0 at home by Newcastle United. In 1913, Womack was innocently involved in a bribery scandal when he was offered the sum of 55 guineas to help 'fix' the Birmingham v Grimsby game so that it would end in a draw. The right-back reported the incident to club officials who set a trap and the culprit was arrested and charged. Womack, who was twice named as non-travelling reserve for the full England team, appeared for the Football League XI in 1918–19. In 1920–21 he helped the Blues win the Second Division Championship and, though he never scored a goal for the club in 515 first-team outings, he liked nothing better than to push upfield and support his forwards. Womack had, however, a most unusual habit – before heading the ball, he would always clap his hands! On leaving St Andrew's, he became player–manager of Worcester City and in his first season with the club, he led them to the Birmingham League title. After two years he took charge of Torquay United before managing Grimsby Town whom he led into the First Division. In October 1936 he took over the reins at Leicester City and led them to promotion from the Second Division at the end of the season. During the war years, he managed Notts County and in 1946 took charge of Oldham Athletic but resigned after just one season in which the Latics came perilously close to having to apply for re-election to the Third Division (North).

WORST STARTS The club's worst-ever start to a season was in 1978–79. It took 14 league games to record the first victory over the season as the Blues drew three and lost ten of the opening fixtures. The run ended with a 5–1 defeat of Manchester United at St Andrew's on 11 November 1978. Despite that victory, the

Frank Worthington

club won only five more matches and were relegated to the Second Division at the end of the campaign.

WORTHINGTON, FRANK Frank Worthington was a talented footballer and an extrovert who began his career with Huddersfield Town. After helping the Terriers win the Second Division Championship in 1970, the chance came for him to join Liverpool. A fee of £150,000 had been agreed but a medical examination revealed that he had high blood pressure and Leicester seized their chance and a cut-price Worthington moved to Filbert Street for £80,000. His elegantly effective centre-forward play was rewarded with an England call-up and he went on to make eight appearances at full international level. He had scored 72 goals in 210 games for the Foxes when, after a spell on loan to Bolton Wanderers, he joined the Trotters on a permanent basis. He became a footballing hero at Burnden Park and soon rediscovered the style which had made him one of the best strikers in the game. In 1977–78 he helped the Wanderers win the Second Division Championship and the following season he ended the campaign with 24 goals to top the First Division goalscoring charts. He had scored 38 goals in 93 games when he moved to Birmingham City for £150,000 in November 1979. He made his début in a 2–1 home defeat against one of his former clubs, Leicester City, and at the end of the season the Blues had won promotion to the First Division with Worthington having scored four goals in 19 league games. In 1980–81 Worthington was the club's top scorer with 18 goals and went on to score 33 in 88 games before leaving to join Leeds United. He later had spells with Sunderland, Southampton, Brighton, Tranmere, Preston and Stockport County. One of the game's most gifted and colourful strikers, he made 757 league appearances in a career that saw him approaching his fortieth birthday before he left the first-class game.

WRIGHT, BILLY A life-long Everton supporter, Billy Wright made his début for the Goodison club as a substitute for George Telfer in a 2–0 home win over Leicester City in February 1978. By the start of the following season, the hard-working defender had established himself in the heart of the Everton defence and was later made club captain. The popular Wright began to put on weight and just hours before a league game at Ipswich Town in December 1982, manager Howard Kendall told his captain he was being left out as a disciplinary measure for weighing 8lbs more than the club allowed! He never played for the Toffees again and six months later, after he had appeared in 198 first-team games, he joined Birmingham City on a free transfer. After making his début for the Blues in a 4–0 defeat at West Ham United on the opening day of the 1983–84 season, Wright went on to play in 40 league games but, despite a number of outstanding performances, he couldn't prevent the club being relegated. He was the only ever-present the following seasons as the Blues returned to the top flight at the first attempt. However, following the appointment of John Bond as Birmingham manager, his future at St Andrew's was more uncertain and after a loan spell with Chester, he ended his league career with Carlisle United.

WYLIE, RON Ron Wylie began his career with Notts County and made his league début against Doncaster Rovers in October 1951. In seven seasons with the Meadow Lane club he scored 33 goals in 227 league games before leaving to join Aston Villa for a fee of £9,250 in November 1958. Linking well with Peter McParland, he helped Villa win the Second Division Championship and League Cup. In 1964–65 he was voted Midland Footballer of the Year. He had scored 27 goals in 245 games when he left Villa Park to join Birmingham City. He made his début for the Blues in a 2–1 home win over Crystal Palace on the opening day of the 1965–66 season. In five seasons at St Andrew's he led the club into the League Cup and FA Cup semi-finals in 1967 and 1968 respectively. He had appeared in 149 league and cup games for the Blues when he left to return to Villa Park as coach, and then to Coventry City, initially as coach and then assistant-manager. Afterwards he went to Cyprus as soccer coach-advisor and was appointed manager of Hong Kong club Bulova before returning to these shores as team manager of West Bromwich Albion in the summer of 1982. He left the Hawthorns in February 1984 to join Villa for a third time as the club's second-team coach, but then lost his job on the appointment of Graham Taylor. Wylie returned to Villa Park as Football in the Community Officer in 1990.

X

'X' In football, 'x' traditionally stands for a draw. The club record for the number of draws in a season was set in seasons 1937–38 and 1971–72 when they drew 18 of their matches.

XMAS DAY There was a time when league matches were regularly played on Christmas Day but in recent years the game's authorities have dropped the fixture from their calendar. The last time Birmingham City played on Christmas Day was 1954 when they lost 1–0 at home to Nottingham Forest in front of a 33,500 crowd. City played a league game on Christmas Day for the first time in 1896 when they drew 3–3 at home to local rivals Walsall. The following season, Walter Abbott netted a hat-trick in a 5–1 home defeat of Darwen. When the Blues beat Stockport County 4–2 at home in 1908, all the club's goals were scored by Fred Chapple in what was only his fourth game. The club's biggest win on Christmas Day came in 1913 when Glossop were beaten 6–0. In 1925 the club's greatest goalscorer, Joe Bradford, scored all three goals in a 3–1 defeat of Tottenham Hotspur, whilst the last Birmingham player to score a hat-trick in a Christmas Day fixture was Bill Smith in a 4–0 home win over Rotherham United.

Y

YOUNGEST PLAYER The youngest player to appear in a first-class fixture for Birmingham City is the club's current manager Trevor Francis who was 16 years and 139 days old when he came on as a substitute for Bob Latchford in the Second Division match against Cardiff City (Away 0–2) on 5 September 1970.

YOUTH CUP Birmingham City have appeared in the FA Youth Cup final on just one occasion. In 1966–67 the Blues met Sunderland in the two-legged final. A crowd of 10,440 saw Birmingham lose 1–0 at home to the Wearsiders, while five days later at Roker Park the scoreline was the same resulting in a Sunderland victory of 2–0 on aggregate.

Z

ZENITH The club enjoyed their best period in the mid-1950s, for after winning the Second Division Championship in 1954–55, the Blues had an excellent season back in the top flight, finishing in sixth place: they achieved their highest final place in the club's history and reached the FA Cup final where they lost 3–1 to Manchester City.